THE ASEAN ECONOMIC COMMUNITY

The Association of Southeast Asian Nations (ASEAN) has experienced rapid economic growth for many years. Although the population of AEAN is larger than that of the EU-28, the emerging ASEAN market, called the ASEAN Economic Community (AEC), is still little understood by policy makers in many parts of the world, by business professionals and students, as well as by scholars in economics, business, politics and economic law. This book provides, for the first time, a rigorous analytical approach to the new AEC and its intricacies. It sets out its ambition, scrutinises its economic integration logic and detects its deficits. Besides providing a detailed analysis of the AEC Roadmap, the book also elaborates on its achievements. Several strategic economic options for the AEC, in particular as an instrument to accelerate the economic development of the region, are explored.

JACQUES PELKMANS is a senior fellow at the Centre for European Policy Studies (CEPS), and professor at the College of Europe. He is a seasoned observer of ASEAN economic integration and has written extensively on it in Asian and European publications. He has had a varied and extensive career which has combined technical as well as conceptual work both on European economic integration and on ASEAN, first on AFTA (the ASEAN free trade area) and later for the ASEAN Economic Community.

INTEGRATION THROUGH LAW

The Role of Law and the Rule of Law in ASEAN Integration

General Editors

J. H. H. Weiler, European University Institute

Tan Hsien-Li, National University of Singapore

The Association of Southeast Asian Nations (ASEAN), comprising the ten member states of Brunei Darussalam, Cambodia, Indonesia, Lao PDR, Malaysia, Myanmar, Philippines, Singapore, Thailand and Vietnam, has undertaken intensified integration into the ASEAN Community through the Rule of Law and Institutions in its 2007 Charter. This innovative book series evaluates the community-building processes of ASEAN to date and offers a conceptual and policy toolkit for broader Asian thinking and planning of different legal and institutional models of economic and political regional integration in the region. Participating scholars have been divided up into six separate thematic strands. The books combine a mix of Asian and Western scholars.

Centre for International Law, National University of Singapore (CIL-NUS)

The Centre for International Law (CIL) was established in 2009 at the National University of Singapore's Bukit Timah Campus in response to the growing need for international law expertise and capacity building in the Asia-Pacific region. CIL is a university-wide research centre that focuses on multidisciplinary research and works with other NUS or external centres of research and academic excellence. In particular, CIL collaborates very closely with the NUS Faculty of Law.

INTEGRATION THROUGH LAW
The Role of Law and the Rule of Law in ASEAN Integration
General Editors: J. H. H. Weiler and Tan Hsien-Li

THE ASEAN ECONOMIC COMMUNITY

A Conceptual Approach

JACQUES PELKMANS

CAMBRIDGE
UNIVERSITY PRESS

CAMBRIDGE
UNIVERSITY PRESS

University Printing House, Cambridge CB2 8BS, United Kingdom

Cambridge University Press is part of the University of Cambridge.

It furthers the University's mission by disseminating knowledge in the pursuit of education, learning and research at the highest international levels of excellence.

www.cambridge.org
Information on this title: www.cambridge.org/9781107590731

First published 2016

A catalogue record for this publication is available from the British Library

ISBN 978-1-107-59073-1 Paperback

CONTENTS

FIGURES

TABLES

BOXES

GENERAL EDITORS' PREFACE

This monograph is published within the context of a wide-ranging research project entitled Integration Through Law: The Role of Law and the Rule of Law in ASEAN Integration (ITL), undertaken by the Centre for International Law at the National University of Singapore and directed by J. H. H. Weiler and Tan Hsien-Li.

The Preamble to the ASEAN Charter concludes with a single decision: 'We, the Peoples of the Member States of the Association of Southeast Asian Nations . . . [h]ereby decide to establish, through this Charter, the legal and institutional framework for ASEAN.' For the first time in its history of over four decades, the Legal and the Institutional were brought to the forefront of ASEAN discourse.

The gravitas of the medium, a Charter: the substantive ambition of its content, the creation of three interlocking Communities, and the turn to law and institutions as instruments for realisation provide ample justification for this wide-ranging project, to which this monograph is one contribution, examining ASEAN in a comparative context.

That same substantive and, indeed, political ambition means that any single study, illuminating as it may be, will cover but a fraction of the phenomena. Our modus operandi in this project was to create teams of researchers from Asia and elsewhere who would contribute individual monographs within an overall framework which we had designed.

The project framework, involving several thematic clusters within each monograph, is thus determined by the framework and the place of each monograph within it.

As regards the specific content, however, the authors were free, indeed encouraged, to define their own understanding of the problem and their own methodology and reach their own conclusions. The thematic structure of the entire project may be found at the end of this Preface.

The project as a whole, and each monograph within it, display several methodological sensibilities.

First, law, in our view, can only be understood and evaluated when situated in its political and economic context. Thus, the first studies in the overall project design are intended to provide the political, economic, cultural and historical context against which one must understand ASEAN and are written by specialists in these respective disciplines. This context, to a greater or lesser degree, also informs the sensibility of each monograph. There are no 'black letter law' studies to be found in this project and, indeed, even in the most technical of areas we encouraged our authors to make their writing accessible to readers of diverse disciplines.

Comparative experience suggests that the success of achieving some of the more ambitious objectives outlined in Article 1 of the Charter will depend in no small measure on the effectiveness of legal principles, legal rules and legal institutions. This is particularly true as regards the success of establishing 'an ASEAN Community comprising the ASEAN Security Community, the ASEAN Economic Community and the ASEAN Socio-Cultural Community as provided for in the Bali Declaration of ASEAN Concord II'. Article 2(2)(n) stipulates the commitment of ASEAN Member States to act in accordance with the principle of 'adherence to multilateral trade rules and ASEAN's rules-based regimes for effective implementation of economic commitments and progressive reduction towards elimination of all barriers to regional economic integration'. The ASEAN Member States therefore envisage that rules of law and the Rule of Law will become a major feature in the future of ASEAN.

Although, as seen, the Charter understands itself as providing an institutional and legal framework for ASEAN, the question of the 'role of law and the rule of law' is not advocacy but a genuine enquiry in the various substantive areas of the project as to:

- the substantive legal principles and substantive rules of the various ASEAN communities;
- the procedural legal principles and rules governing institutional structures and decision-making processes;
- implementation, enforcement and dispute settlement.

One should not expect a mechanical application of this scheme in each study; rather, a sensibility that refuses to content itself with legal enactments as such and looks to a 'living' notion of law and institutions is ubiquitous in all the studies. Likewise, the project is sensitive to 'non Law'. It variously attempts to locate the appropriate province of the law in this experience. That is, not only the role of law, but also the areas that are and should remain outside the reach of legal institutionalisation with due sensitivity to ASEAN and Asian particularism and political and cultural identities.

The project, and the monographs of which it is made, are not normatively thick. They do not advocate. They are designed, for the most part, to offer reflection, discuss the pros and cons, and in this way enrich public awareness, deepen understanding of different options and in that respect contribute indirectly to policymaking.

This decisive development of ASEAN has been accompanied by a growing Asian interest in various legal and institutional forms of transnational economic and political cooperation, notably the various voices discussing and showing an interest in an East Asia Integration project. The number of Free Trade Agreements (FTAs) and Regional Trade Agreements (RTAs) has increased from six in 1991 to 166 in 2013, with a further 62 in various stages of negotiations.

Methodologically, the project and many of the monographs are comparative in their orientation. Comparative law is one of the few real-life laboratories that we have in which to assess and understand the operation of different legal and institutional models designed to tackle similar objectives and problems. One should not need to put one's own hand in the fire to learn that it scorches. With that in mind a couple of monographs offer both conceptual reflection and pragmatic 'tool boxing' on some of the key elements featuring in all regional integration systems.

Comparative law is in part about divergence: it is a potent tool and means to understand one's own uniqueness. One understands better the uniqueness of apples by comparing them to oranges. You understand better the specialness of a Toyota by comparing it to a Ford.

Comparative law is also about convergence: it is a potent tool and means to understand how what are seemingly different phenomena are part of a broader trend, an insight which may enhance both self-understanding and policy potentialities.

Although many studies in the project could have almost immediate policy implications, as would the project as a whole, this is not its only or even principal purpose. There is a rich theory of federalism which covers many countries around the world. There is an equally rich theory of European integration, which has been associated with the advent of the Union. There is also considerable learning on Free Trade Areas and the like.

To date, the study of the legal aspects of ASEAN specifically and other forms of Asian legal integration has been derivative of, and dependent on, theoretical and conceptual insights which were developed in different contexts.

One principal objective of ITL and these monographs will be to put in place the building blocks for an authentic body of ASEAN and Asian integration theory developed in, and with sensitivity to, the particularities and peculiarities of the region and continent. A theory and conceptual framework of Asian legal integration will signal the coming of age of research of and in the region itself.

Although the monographs form part of an overarching project, we asked our authors to write each as a 'stand-alone' – not assuming that their readers would have consulted any of the other titles. Indeed, the project is rich and few will read all monographs. We encourage readers to pick and choose from the various monographs and design their own menu. There is, on occasion, some overlap in providing, for example, background information on ASEAN in different studies. That is not only inevitable but desirable in a project of this amplitude.

The world is increasingly witnessing a phenomenon of interlocking regional organisations where the experience of one feeds on the others. In some way, the intellectual, disciplinary and comparative sensibility of this project is a microcosm of the world it describes.

The range of topics covered in this series comprises:

The General Architecture and Aspirations of ASEAN
The Governance and Management of ASEAN: Instruments, Institutions, Monitoring, Compliance and Dispute Resolution
Legal Regimes in ASEAN
The ASEAN Economic Community
ASEAN and the World
The Substantive Law of ASEAN

Chapter 1

Introduction and purpose[1]

Understanding ASEAN's economic integration model is a genuine challenge. A fundamental reason why conceptual and other difficulties arise in the case of the ASEAN Economic Community (AEC) is that ASEAN architects observe two stylised (regional) economic integration approaches in the world which they do *not* want to pursue: the 'EU model', which is supranational, far too ambitious and also to a degree 'open-ended' in terms of further ambitions, and the classical free trade area (FTA) approach, even when upgraded a little nowadays. Another reason for conceptual puzzles is found in ASEAN's strategic (development) preference of hooking up to global value chains, without a firm view on how such a strategy relates to 'deep' economic integration. Within the framework of the ASEAN Integration through Law project, the purpose of the present monograph is to try to make the ASEAN economic integration model intelligible

[1] The author is indebted to J. H. H. Weiler, Michael Ewing-Chow, Hsien-Li Tan, and several participants of the Singapore workshop for constructive comments and useful queries which stimulated some further thinking as well as improvements of the draft text at the time. Above all, however, I am grateful to my colleague Siow Yue Chia, who, as a careful reader and discussant of the draft version, raised many interesting points and cautioned not to read too much sophistication into some puzzling ASEAN decisions and indeed the absence of decisions in other instances. It goes without saying that the present author is solely responsible for whatever flaws or errors remain.

by applying a *conceptual* approach. This conceptual approach is drawn out in considerable detail, but it is also 'tested' by providing a wealth of factual detail about how ASEAN implements the AEC. The merit of the conceptual approach is, above all, that the numerous technical and often highly specific measures, as well as the many ASEAN 'principles' and 'guidelines', not to speak of detailed Roadmaps, can be understood in context and their economic and practical significance for market players better appreciated. Given the ASEAN 'way' of building up commitments, whether for the former AFTA or now for the AEC, it is exceedingly difficult to make (over 500) elements of the AEC Roadmap intelligible and give them a 'place'. However, right from the start, it is crucial to appreciate that the AEC is based on two concepts, presented as parallel: the 'single market' and (ASEAN as a) 'production base' for segments of global value chains. Whereas the single ASEAN market has at least been defined with respect to some key properties (such as 'free flows'), this is not the case for the 'production base'. It is also exceedingly difficult to trace authoritative statements about, let alone a legal basis for, the political priority of one concept over the other, or how the two concepts are linked, say, by some minimum overlap of measures or otherwise. This generates a profound problem for this monograph: in focusing on the ASEAN economic integration model, we risk reading more into 'the' single market than might be warranted, for the simple reason that ASEAN's implicit development aims are overriding and this may well prompt a bias towards the 'production base'. The greater the bias in favour of the 'production base', the greater the temptation for ASEAN decision makers to regard the single market programme as serving the 'production base' as well, thereby rendering the single market programme less coherent and more difficult to comprehend in terms of integration logic. Stronger, this lesser coherence or greater incompleteness or selectivity in addressing problems which, in an integration strategy, would need to be tackled convincingly, might not even be seen as a problem by ASEAN leaders or business. What might matter most to them is a medium or even long-run growth prospect for the region and, if the production base is expected to be growth-enhancing in a powerful way (as experience in East Asia suggests), the single market as a 'concept' may well be downgraded in actual practice. Since global value chains thrive on 'openness' of economies and easy market access (in particular, in East Asia), market access in East Asia via FTAs might rank as high or higher for the success of the ASEAN production base than the pursuit of an ever deeper – indeed, 'single' – internal ASEAN market. The present monograph will focus on the ASEAN economic integration logic from a conceptual point of view, but the intricate and multifold linkages with measures relevant for ASEAN as a 'production base' cannot be left out.

The ASEAN Economic Community might be called a 'vision' if one reads the 2003 Bali Concord. It contains plenty of conceptual elements which can be analysed separately as well as jointly. Nevertheless, when going from an avowed 'vision' to the scrutiny of what exactly the AEC is and/or is meant to be, it becomes harder to comprehend its concepts, the way(s) they hang together and its 'final' economic integration 'model'. Perhaps this is not surprising. The 'ASEAN way' has never given primacy, so far, to logic and rigorous conceptual models, but usually amounts to pragmatic responses – mainly to external pressures – and under political constraints such as far-reaching respect for national sovereignty and a search for consensus. The initial approach, quite general at the outset, is typically refined or 'deepened' later, again pragmatically, step by step, and taking care that consensus is not undermined. Of course, the present study will not ignore such constraints and traditions.

Nevertheless, the queries addressed are conceptual. The justification for conceptual analysis and scrutinising integration logic is that economic integration, and even more so 'deep' economic integration, can tolerate only limited degrees of incompleteness and only so many inconsistencies. Not only are 'half-way houses' and serious inconsistencies affecting the credibility of integration with business and citizens – once credibility is lost, the entire integration attempt might well become pointless from an economic point of view – they will also generate never ending pressures, frictions and perhaps even tensions which might eventually sap the energies needed for intense cooperation and convergence. Indeed, in ASEAN, economically so dependent on the world economy and more and more on East Asia, national political and negotiating energies might instead be spent on deeper relations with external partners.

The present contribution to the ASEAN Integration through Law project aims to scrutinise the concepts, logic, sequencing, coherence and options for the 2015 AEC. This is supplemented by extensive scrutiny of what has actually been accomplished (and not) for realising the AEC, until recently. The author will assume an economic perspective, whilst taking due account of institutional, legal and political economy aspects where essential. Economic integration processes largely take place in markets. Nevertheless, it is difficult to escape from the notion that a political desire to pursue (ever) 'deeper' economic integration requires (ever) more demanding regulatory, economic policy, political and institutional as well as legal commitments by participating countries. Building on the ASEAN Free Trade Area (AFTA), a classical FTA based on (practically) zero intra-AFTA tariffs and liberal origin rules, the pursuit of an AEC will significantly raise ambition and widen the scope of the policy spectrum for economic integration. This is bound to extend decision-making from trade (and 'ASEAN') ministers to broader government policies and reforms of standing economic regulation practices. Assuring 'deeper' economic integration is therefore very different in nature than fixing a classical FTA. It must imply domestic reforms and possibly a shift to regulatory regimes distinct from those applied today in ASEAN countries, besides the acceptance of a range of ASEAN 'disciplines' going far beyond those of the GATT and GATS.

The book has seven chapters. Following this introductory chapter, Chapter 2 deals with the foundations of economic integration. It will discuss five 'fundamentals', recall the modern version of the 'stages approach' to economic integration and its relevance for the AEC, and address the intricate yet critical issue of credibility and transparency to market players. Going into the foundations is inspired by the 'vision' and labelling of the conceptual elements of the AEC, toying with some of the constituting elements of the 1957 EEC (Rome Treaty). But it can also be read as a stand-alone reflection. Chapter 2 also addresses the strategic choices and economic rationales of the AEC. First, the AEC and NAFTA are compared in section 2.4 as to four strategic choices for the integration model. The main query is whether the AEC can develop an equally compelling integration logic as that of NAFTA, hinging on the answers to those four strategic choices. In section 2.5, the query is what are the economic rationales for the AEC, in particular given its pursuit of its medium- and long-term socio-economic aims. Two partly overlapping economic perspectives will be reviewed: one economic rationale is an ASEAN-led development strategy rendering ASEAN more attractive for global value chains, the other is a quasi-single market strategy as a pro-competitive underpinning of economic development. Chapter 3 is driven by the question 'what exactly is the AEC?' Discovering what the AEC is may be regarded as a descriptive exercise – which it is, no doubt – but it will also require quite some exegesis and interpretation. Section 3.1 recalls and stylises the Bali Concord and the High Level Task Force (HLTF) recommendations. In section 3.2 an attempt is made to grasp the contents and economic meaning of the Bali 'vision' on the basis of a series of conceptual questions. Section 3.3 discusses the five economic concepts of the Bali AEC 'vision', whereas section 3.4 provides a summary of the AEC Roadmap drawn up several years after Bali. Chapter 4 zooms in on the 'hard core' of the AEC in the Roadmap, taking into account the progress made in implementing the plans up to spring 2013. Since the Roadmap is a lengthy document with nearly 300 steps in many domains, the analysis amounts to a painstaking exercise for the reader, yet it is indispensable for a profound understanding of the substance of the AEC as foreseen by its architects. The exercise demonstrates that it is difficult, indeed somewhat arbitrary, to attribute the various Roadmap features to the ASEAN single market or to ASEAN as a regional production base. It also shows that the AEC strategy has compelled ASEAN to work on its complexity and sub-agendas much more than was perhaps foreseen at the Bali ASEAN summit. Chapter 5 provides a reality check by comparing the ASEAN AEC with NAFTA in greater detail. The comparison is made with the help of a lengthy table for fifteen of the main areas of the NAFTA treaty, compared with the status for these areas in the AEC (with quite some detail per area) and a brief comparison with the EU as well. The table helps to demonstrate that the AEC and NAFTA are not far apart, except for a few areas where ASEAN would have to raise its credibility. Chapter 6 suggests three stylised options for the AEC, close enough to the 'vision'. The idea is to obtain coherence within every stylised option and to consider some trade-offs. The term 'economic integration model' should be understood in a flexible way, given ASEAN's strong preference for more and higher value-added participation in global value chains enabled via its regional production base. Chapter 7 concludes.

Chapter 2

Foundations of economic integration fundamentals, stages and credibility

In attempting to understand the AEC and grasp its full potential as well as its limitations, it is indispensable to first go through a careful identification of the foundations of its possible economic integration model. We shall do this by: (a) articulating the fundamentals of any economic integration and discussing their relevance to the AEC; (b) linking the (modern) stages approach to economic integration to the AEC 'vision'; and (c) addressing the intricate, yet critical, issue of credibility and transparency to market players.

2.1 Fundamentals of economic integration and the AEC

When (regional) 'economic integration' is intended to move significantly beyond, say, a classical FTA in goods, it becomes more and more crucial to first appreciate several fundamentals. A non-exhaustive list of such fundamentals includes: (i) the political framework; (ii) the long-term commitment of the participating countries, expressed in credible treaties or otherwise; (iii) the level of development and/or the disparities in prosperity and capabilities; (iv) the 'economic order', in particular, the respect for market-driven incentives; and (v) some form of implicit or explicit consensus on the comprehensiveness or selectivity of economic integration.

2.1.1 *The political framework*

For 'deeper' economic integration to be meaningful, governments and political leaders have to assume a long-term perspective. They have to be seen as willing to accept, at least to a non-trivial degree, the domestic consequences of 'deeper' integration. A failure to do so will not only leave major gaps or omissions in what that Member State is committing to, but will reduce, at the same time, the preparedness of partners to further the process. It will equally damage credibility with market players, who have to exploit the promised opportunities and generate the prosperity gains sought. Of course, socio-economic and political sensitivities are a reality almost everywhere in the world, and various formulae can and will be employed to cope with such problems. One may mention agreed exceptions, exemptions and delays, though all of these run into their natural limits – otherwise the economic integration pursued will simply not emerge. One may allow the ASEAN-X formula, or (what Europeans call) 'géométrie variable' or differentiated integration, but these cannot be pushed too far and will eventually have to be addressed, if not overcome, to a considerable extent. With all the finesse and variations in the integration process between governments, there is no escape from the dictum that the political framework required for significantly 'deeper' economic integration has to be sufficiently firm and credible. Insisting on 'sovereignty' (whatever that means in today's world economy) as an *a priori* for many policy domains affected by deeper integration basically amounts to a denial of the 'depth' of economic integration. For ASEAN countries, claims of nation-building and national development strategies are understandable, and their resonance with the electorate is probably still great. This artefact renders 'deeper' economic integration, already difficult by its very nature, even more challenging for ASEAN countries.

In Eurospeak, the insistence on an 'intergovernmental' approach, driven by widely felt preferences to retain a great deal of national economic policy autonomy, risks being at odds with the very goal pursued. The AEC will have to cope with this fundamental question not only today (in 2015), but also later. Employing intergovernmentalism for the AEC has three distinct (though related) aspects, and all three have to be carefully considered: (a) intergovernmentalism is politically heavy-going and slow, in particular, when there are no overarching 'mother principles' to which all Member States are bound and can be held accountable; (b) relying on intergovernmentalism *without* having, at the same time, carefully construed forms and capabilities of integration which are centralised is much harder than a well-considered combination of centralised and intergovernmental decision-making – this combination has the great advantage that the remaining degrees of national economic autonomy tend to be well protected (which is what national politics wants to see), whilst the cumbersome search for consensus does not affect the hard core of 'deeper' economic integration any longer; (c) intergovernmentalism is also inefficient, if not outright impractical or ineffective, in terms of administration, monitoring, the universe of technical and other regulatory issues at the detailed level (from standards, certification, other conformity assessment assurances, specifics of regulation in network industries and, for example, food laws, medicines, diploma recognition, details of financial supervision, etc.), implementation at the national level (subject to bureaucratic, political or judicial review?), avoidance of dispute settlement by effective and speedy consultation, and coping with functional pressures to amend regulatory or liberalisation measures already taken, which are bound to come and multiply over time. What these considerations would seem to imply is that ASEAN is well advised to reflect seriously about the suitability of its political framework and the political 'axiomas' of its Member States for the building and operation of the AEC. If one would not opt for any significant change after such a thorough reflection, at least one will better appreciate the gaps and stumbling blocks on the road to 'deeper' economic integration. Perhaps ASEAN will be capable of finding imperfect but workable substitutes of more straightforward centralisation, which leave intergovernmentalism fully in place, but with some 'soft' constraints removing the worst inefficiencies, a controlled quasi-delegation to the ASEAN secretariat for 'technical' initiatives and cautious progress in transparency and monitoring by agencies or bodies independent of national governments.

2.1.2 *Long-term legal or other commitments*

Although ASEAN countries, as well as ASEAN as a group, have concluded many treaties, and have recently ratified the

ASEAN Charter, the debate on the degree and reliability of the participating countries' commitment to the AEC and its consequences for detailed measures and/or liberalisation of intra-ASEAN market access has never stopped.[1] However, it would be a mistake to regard the degree and credibility of 'binding' for ASEAN countries, for example, in implementation and in sanctioning the violation of earlier ASEAN decisions, as a pure legal question. 'Deeper' economic integration hinges on the credibility and reliability of AEC-related decisions and their effective (and sufficiently homogeneous) implementation. Long-term legal (or other credible) commitment and its enforcement is crucial for economic operators, whether ASEAN-based or global. Multinationals and ASEAN's internationalising firms will cast a judgement on these matters, year after year. True, such experienced and capable firms can live with restrictions and hindrances, as long as it is still attractive enough for their business. But as the very purpose of the AEC is to attract more foreign direct investment (FDI), to increase local value-added in global value chains, and to generate additional prosperity by moving up the dynamic comparative advantage and quality ladder in a fiercely competitive setting in East Asia and beyond, the credibility of the AEC and effective results are critical for

[1] The ASEAN Integration through Law project has paid considerable attention to the significance of law, the nature of commitments, and the rigour and reliability of implementation by ASEAN countries. See, e.g., the papers by Beckman *et al.* (2013); Dehousse and Aziz (2013); Inama and Sim (2013a); Peng, Hix and Chalermpalanupap (2013); Tan and Dann (2013); Weiler and Ewing-Chow (2013); Weiler (2013).

generating these economic benefits. This would be equally true for commitments leading to a single market.

2.1.3 Level of development and disparities in the group

Practically all significant instances of regional economic integration beyond simple, classical FTAs are confronted with the issue of disparities in levels of development of their member countries. Think of NAFTA, ASEAN itself, the old EFTA (with Portugal), the original East African customs union, the EU or the Southern African Customs Union. Major disparities may have lasting consequences for the depth of economic integration and the speed of progress, as well as for the political balance amongst member countries. Another fundamental aspect of economic regionalism is the overall level of development of the group. It is widely known that a group of developing countries (South/South) is unlikely to find that its economic development objectives are successfully realised via integration in its own region for reasons of similarity of goods structure, the still modest attractiveness for global value chains, the risk of trade diversion, and the much higher priority of gaining market access to OECD countries where most demand is (still) concentrated. Highly developed and diversified economies, on the other hand, are likely to gain statically and dynamically in many ways if the design of economic integration is appropriate. With many ASEAN countries having arrived at middle income status and only three members struggling to get there, the political incentives for ASEAN to 'deepen' integration and to articulate dynamic comparative advantages have undoubtedly increased during the last decade or so. It should give confidence to political leaders, but just as much to local business, when pursuing the long and complex road to the AEC. In turn, a fully-fledged AEC as expressed in both aims is likely to stimulate development in an international context even further and prompt the transformation of national economies helped by strong economic growth.

2.1.4 The 'economic order' or the roles of markets and government

Allowing permanently 'deep' forms of market access and significant constraints on domestic government intervention, be it at the border or 'behind the border', presupposes some (perhaps implicit) consensus on the 'economic order'. The economic order can be defined as the systemic relation between markets and the multiple roles of government in order for the economy to support the pursuit of certain general, often politically formulated, goals in the longer run. Even though most economies nowadays are 'market economies', this does not mean that the market–government relationship in all the countries is the same or even somewhat similar. This is neither the case amongst OECD countries, nor in ASEAN or elsewhere. However, when there is a degree of convergence or, put differently, when there are not too many or too wide political or ideological policy domains or types of intervention that are 'non-negotiable', the initial steps towards 'deeper' economic integration should be feasible. Nevertheless, with further 'deepening' of market-driven integration, a greater degree of convergence will inevitably be required. It might also be forced upon participating countries as an outcome of the process. The EU provides two telling examples. First, in co-founding the 1958 EEC, France was de facto giving up its postwar 'dirigiste' system of running the economy, with sectoral committees mixing business and government, strong powers of intervention for the government, significant government ownership of companies and considerable political control or influence. This system was quietly and gradually dismantled while the economy was opening up, interventionism was curtailed step by step (via EU measures and EU obligations for France), and national as well as EU competition policy was developed. Second, after the fall of communism in Europe, Central and Eastern European countries experienced a radical transformation of the economic order, at first more on paper than in actual economic practice. What seemed impossible and unreal in, say, 1988, happened only a few years later: these countries were eager to become EU members and initiated various association agreements almost immediately after 1990, precisely to render their new economic order more robust and to benefit from the prosperity gains this would yield. Thus, the convergence between their fragile economic order and that of the EU became ever stronger by design and by huge efforts undertaken via so-called 'pre-accession' (i.e., preparation for EU membership).

It should not surprise anyone that ASEAN countries hope for an evolution analogous to that of France in the early days of the EEC. Such accommodation processes are profoundly political and ought to be given time for domestic debate and gradual adjustment. Speaking generalities is no cure for what ultimately has to be achieved as a minimum to enable 'deeper' economic integration to be meaningful. Nevertheless, France was helped in this accommodation by the uncompromising 'mother principles' in the EEC Treaty it had itself ratified and the powers of the central EU institutions. The 'mother principles' of the EEC were made less ambivalent by European Court of Justice (CJEU) case law and a partial rewrite of the EEC Treaty in 1985. Absent central judicial review in ASEAN and assuming that the AEC is the 'final' destination of ASEAN, the necessary accommodation processes are bound to take much longer and may actually remain 'stuck' or otherwise be too partial and selective for 'deeper' economic integration to be credible and ASEAN-wide.

2.1.5 Comprehensiveness or selectivity in the AEC

The idea of comprehensiveness does not necessarily depend on the ticking-off of long lists of 'actions' in 'roadmaps'. We hasten to stress that roadmaps can be a most useful practical device for promoting concrete progress and transparency, whilst forming a basic, objective tool to hold all ASEAN Member States accountable during the AEC formation process. But comprehensiveness crucially hinges on the underlying concept of what an AEC means and what it is supposed to accomplish. Not unlike tariff lines at the six-digit level that can be refined to numerous eight-, nine- and ten-digit tariff lines (often for protectionist purposes), roadmaps can be refined and their specific actions made ever more trivial. With such evasive practices, one risks confusing the many trees for the forest. What matters first is the design, hence the underlying (economic) *concept*, of the AEC. If the design is too selective, the 'depth' of economic integration will not be believed by market players and the gains of such a regional 'deepening' may well remain limited. Insofar as the Roadmap is the concrete expression of the AEC design, it will have to be subjected to a conceptual analysis, which is what the present author sets out to do (see section 3.3.). There might well be a further implication. With roadmaps being used as a tool to guide and stimulate the building of the AEC, the hidden weaknesses and omissions will come to the surface sooner or later, be it inside the negotiation process or due to pressures from prominent investors or business at large. If selectivity is too dominant and the design unconvincing, two things might happen which are not formally addressed right now: (a) the AEC-building as foreseen may have to shift its deadline for completion beyond 2015, indeed, shift it repeatedly; and (b) it is also plausible that the very process of AEC-building itself will eventually help to inspire a re-think of the original AEC design, for example, reducing selectivity and strengthening its degree of binding for ASEAN Member States. This will be the more likely the greater the pressure to remain attractive and competitive globally and, in particular, in East Asia or Asia overall. Now that the deadline of 2015 is approaching, a new follow-up programme for 2015–2025 is being formulated on request of the ASEAN leaders. The decisian on this programme is expected to be taken in November 2015. Moreover, a kind of 're-think' is at least suggested by the ASEAN Summit in Brunei in 2013, asking for a 'post-2015 Vision' of the AEC before the 2015 AEC deadline.

2.2 The stages of economic integration and the AEC 'vision'

The 2003 Bali Declaration on the AEC is a fascinating document. Whilst ASEAN is not interested in copying the EU model or even echoing its approach in a somewhat weaker form, the declaration nevertheless reads like the 'second life' of the European Economic Community, ASEAN-style. The very name is ASEAN Economic Community, the term free movement seems to be dubbed as 'free flow' and it comprises a single market. These labels are highly suggestive of an economic integration approach reminiscent of the classical stages approach long employed in economic textbooks. We shall therefore begin to verify the conceptual elements of the Bali 'vision' by recalling the classical stages approach of economic integration and attempt to adapt it in two ways: one is to modernise the approach, because the early ideas from around 1960 suffer from gaps and omissions as well as 'vertical incoherence' between some stages; the other is to adapt it to ASEAN and its current predicament. The stages approach attempts to specify in steps the logic of 'deepening' the commitments as well as 'widening' the policy scope of economic integration. Deepening refers to both 'negative' and 'positive' (market) integration, terms going back to the famous first ever book on economic integration by Nobel Laureate Jan Tinbergen (1954).[2] These terms have nothing to do with negative or positive welfare gains, but rather with the design

[2] Tinbergen's first edition of this book, from 1945, still employed the label 'international economic cooperation'. The revised 1954 version is more suitable to analyse modern integration approaches.

of economic integration and the requirements for member states in pursuing more ambitious market integration. 'Negative integration' refers to cross-border (intra-group) liberalisation of market access and, hence, denotes the removal of discrimination or other barriers to the composing national markets. Such barriers can be at the border or 'behind the border'. Such removal ('negative') of requirements for member states stems from an agreement to improve market access inside the group. 'Positive integration', instead, refers to *joint* action by the member states, be it economic cooperation, common economic instruments (such as a common external tariff or a common quota), common regulation (including harmonisation and explicit mutual recognition), and various forms and ambitions of common institutions, possibly with powers delegated from the member states. The treaty design for positive *and* negative integration is likely to be regarded as more sensitive and intrusive by member states than an agreement for negative integration alone. Dependent on what the scope and substance of the joint actions and/or powers of the group would be, and even more so when common institutions with delegated powers are foreseen, this sensitivity and intrusiveness can move over a very wide spectrum indeed. Rendering positive integration credible will require a carefully drafted and balanced treaty in order to be acceptable to national parliaments and voters when up for ratification. The ranges of depth of negative integration and the possible combinations with (which degrees of) positive integration is what the stages approach is all about. The seminal contribution of Balassa (1961) with his five stages of economic integration is reproduced in the Appendix, with annotations and brief comments about some fundamental problems of his approach for a modern design of market integration.[3]

Table 2.1 provides a modern stages approach. It avoids the pitfalls of the classical approach and incorporates newer hybrid versions with greater relevance for all market integration attempts in the world, other than that of the EU. This makes it more suitable for ASEAN as well. A specific adaptation relevant for ASEAN and the AEC is that the most ambitious stages of economic integration, moving even beyond 'deep' market integration, namely, forms of 'economic and monetary union' (EMU), have been left out. Types of EMU are outside the ambitions of ASEAN and there is no point bringing in the complexities of such higher stages.

Table 2.1 begins with two lower stages, the FTA and the CU in the classical sense of GATT, Article 24. The CU is attributed a slightly higher status of ambition because it implies two modest instances of positive integration given the common external tariffs. Nevertheless, one may wonder whether a customs union will necessarily be seen as the next step after an FTA. In ASEAN informal attempts have been undertaken to transform the AFTA into a customs union (with Singapore and possibly Brunei in a special position, obviously), but they seem

[3] In short, Balassa (1961) only introduces 'positive integration' in his fourth stage (economic union), which is logically impossible; he ignored services in his common market definition, and his fifth stage, denoted as 'total economic integration', is highly centralist, without any economic foundation for this. See Pelkmans (1980, 2006, ch. 1) for extensive analysis of these points. Note that Balassa (1976) has revised his earlier views in the light of the debate. See also Sapir (2011) for a recent interpretation of Balassa.

Table 2.1 *A modern stages approach to market integration*

Stage	Definition	Characteristics/notes
Free trade area (FTA)	Tariffs and quotas abolished for intra-area goods imports. Area members retain national tariffs and quotas against third countries.	Classical GATT definition of FTA, de facto, little attention to other barriers, no positive integration.
Customs union (CU)	No tariffs and quotas for intra-area goods imports. Common external tariffs (and common quotas) vis-à-vis third countries. Free goods circulation in area after passing one customs of the group.	Classical GATT definition of CU, de facto, little attention to other barriers, no positive integration, except (a) sharing tariff revenue, (b) common tariff negotiations (for WTO or FTAs).
FTA-plus (or CU-plus)	As the GATT now covers many trade aspects, other than tariffs/quotas, FTAs and CUs must follow and go much beyond stages 1 or 2 (see note 1 below for specifications of eleven WTO agreements+ dispute settlement), also, the GATS and TRIPs agreements add to the 'plus' of FTA/CU plus; many FTAs nowadays strive to be WTO-plus, i.e., go further than WTO	Modern FTAs (and CUs such as the EU–Turkey CU) are WTO-compatible, i.e., incorporate all or most of column 2; few are genuinely WTO-plus, except very selectively, or some sections remain dormant (as in the EU–Turkey CU); in particular, the GATS links tend to be weak due to weak GATS commitments, and the TBT and

Table 2.1 (cont.)

Stage	Definition	Characteristics/notes
	obligations; often, soft economic cooperation is added as well.	SPS elements are minimal, and do not or hardly lead to positive integration.
Deep and comprehensive FTAs/CUs	Ranges from more radically WTO-plus, especially in services, all the way to additional obligations in areas such as investment, competition policy, trade facilitation, forceful equivalence efforts/clauses in TBT issues and selective SPS + economic cooperation and capacity-building; also may incorporate areas under WTO plurilaterals, such as government procurement (or beyond it).	When deep and comprehensive, the FTAs/CUs become intrusive for domestic regulation and certain 'national' policies; this may lead to modest forms of positive integration (e.g., joint monitoring, equivalence of standards or rules, joint committees with de facto rule-making power, compulsory prior consultation, arbitration, judicial dispute settlement).
Common market	A common market consists of free market access in goods, services, labour and capital; as the label suggests, the crucial difference between stage 4 and 5 is found in the fundamental obligation of member states to ensure such access via a combination of negative and positive integration (negative integration alone can never realise such access); thus, the	Common markets are quite an ambitious idea; rather than negotiating to 'open up' sub-markets in a cautious and sensitive process while carving out (or fully reserving) what is too sensitive, the common market is based on blanket open access obligations in all four relevant markets, and what is negotiated are the exceptions, conditionalities, timing, forms

depth of common markets depend on how far member states are willing to go in positive integration to render legally free market access also truly 'effective'; in turn, this hinges on how strict the legal access obligations are formulated, on the exceptions, on the extent and precision of common regulation (etc.) and on joint, credible enforcement.

An option making for a higher ambition is to have a common competition (in fact, anti-trust) policy for the common market so as to improve its proper functioning (here, without undue market power or other private distortions of competition).

Another option to be considered is to have some joint funding in a common budget for purposes of cross-border infrastructure and/or common adjustment support.

and methods of common regulation or approximation of laws, equivalence provisions, etc.; the common institutions need to be granted at least some powers to drive the complicated and often technical process, ensure effective decision-making and guarantee judicial enforcement; the core questions to ask are how straightforward and credible the access obligations and the provisions for positive integration are in the treaty, and whether there is (qualified) majority voting rather than a veto system.

Table 2.1 (cont.)

Stage	Definition	Characteristics/notes
Single market	A single market is an economic concept (see also section 3.3.2 in this monograph); using it as an objective requires defining it operationally, which opens up a wide range of options; as a proxy, it refers to an general intolerance of exceptions to the market access obligations, an intolerance for unequal or poor enforcement, for lingering barriers even if (justifiable) domestic regulation, a wider application of competition policy (including network industries and state aids), a wider view of distortions (e.g., corporate tax base, distinct liability rules, rigorous regimes for state-owned enterprises, hidden restrictions in, e.g., insurance contracts for safety standards etc.); this must imply far-reaching common	The term 'single' causes it to be an extremely ambitious concept for a two-tier governmental system of the integrating area; it need not and should not be centralising in so many respects, but where the lower tier of government retains regulatory discretion, and freedom in budget spending, there should always be a discipline of not distorting or frustrating the single market; even federal countries have not accomplished truly single markets; for countries desiring a single market without common government, the weight necessarily shifts to maintain strict disciplines and hard enforcement, thereby obviating greater centralisation; the practical understanding of a

	regulation and strong powers for common institutions; costly initiatives for more common infrastructure in energy, roads, digital networks, etc. may equalise trade costs in the single market (and improve market functioning); in extreme cases, distinct regulation of (national) labour markets might be reduced or disciplined. In addition, a fifth market is included, that of codified technology and knowledge (usually, IPRs), which may be harmonised or even (partly?) centralised.	single market is therefore always a 'workable' compromise.

[1] The WTO has concluded agreements on agriculture (e.g., support and export subsidies), SPS, TBTs, TRIMs, anti-dumping, textiles and clothing, customs valuation, pre-shipment inspection, rules of origin, import licensing, subsidies and countervailing duties, and safeguards.

[2] In all stages, but especially as from stage 3 upwards, regional market integration is typically accompanied by extensive 'soft' cooperation as per the OECD or APEC, and/or voluntary policy emulation/approximation or best-practice leadership efforts.

[3] The table assumes that all area members adhere to obligations of negative and positive integration in all stages where relevant. However, in all stages there may well be (temporarily or permanently) elements of 'differentiated integration', i.e., some countries have timetables which allow delays or some areas are carved out for some countries (opt-outs). One formula that ASEAN applies is the ASEAN-X approach for policy domains which are sensitive.

to have come to nothing. Not only are customs unions rare in the world economy,[4] the idea of turning an FTA into a customs union is even more rare. A clear case is the EU–Turkey customs union of 1996, following decades of an association based on an FTA. The other well-known instance, Mercosur, is an ambivalent one. The AEC as foreseen will remain a FTA, with lots of additions and modern market access aspects, in other words, stage 3 or higher in Table 3.1. Nevertheless, once participating countries agree on ambitious 'deepening', the question remains whether an FTA is the appropriate basis. The drawback of certificates of origin, requiring proof of nowadays complicated value-added per country or region, remains considerable even with the liberal ASEAN origin rules. With the external tariffs of ASEAN countries having come down since the birth of AFTA, it is well known that business often prefers to avoid the costs of the old form D by relying on most-favoured-nation (MFN) tariff treatment (McKinsey 2003; Manchin and Pelkmans-Balaoing 2008).[5] Because the 'Single Window' would reduce the costs of going through customs irrespective of exploiting AFTA or MFN treatment, keeping the FTA would appear to bring no advantages in the longer run. In a customs union, goods would, after a *single* customs clearance anywhere in ASEAN, come into 'free circulation' in the ASEAN area,

[4] Except for examples of micro countries such as Monaco (via France, with the EU) and Liechtenstein with Switzerland, which are irrelevant for present purposes.

[5] There are several other reasons for the low utilisation rates of AFTA preferences, such as low preferential margins, initially unclear criteria for ASEAN origin and, for example, tariff drawbacks for multinationals. See also Inama and Sim (2013b) for extensive analysis.

which is more attractive and simpler for business. On the other hand, a customs union implies a common external tariff (CET) for all goods, as well as some minimum common machinery to manage it and conducting a common commercial diplomacy in the WTO and/or with trading partners bilaterally or regionally. This may well be sensitive for industrial development or agricultural reasons in some types of goods. Indeed, ASEAN is characterised by great diversity and a CET would be hard to negotiate and would be full of 'holes'.[6] It might also be considered as a form of unwanted centralisation, possibly dominated by Indonesia given its mere size or by the big four (Indonesia, Philippines, Thailand and Vietnam). If tariff convergence is insufficiently advanced and/or exception lists are still too sensitive, a CET may not be feasible in the short to medium term. As indicated, there is also the tricky question of the sharing of tariff revenue. But there may well be a wider implication of sticking to an FTA in the AEC. If a minimum common machinery needed for a customs union is seen as going too far, it might foreshadow repeated difficulties when addressing non-tariff barriers (NTBs) or non-tariff measures (NTMs) seriously. The notion of effectively overcoming technical or other regulatory barriers in goods and services trade without at least having some common machinery, if not selective harmonisation, is almost certainly illusionary.[7]

[6] Such a punctuated CET is the main characteristic of the Mercosur customs union.

[7] A sophisticated treatise on this fundamental problem is given by Sykes (1995), and the contrast with the EU method of removing such barriers is set out by Pelkmans (1995) in the same book.

Nevertheless, despite the FTA status of ASEAN, hence without a common tariff and without a common trade policy, ASEAN countries as a group have succeeded in negotiating several FTA 'frameworks' with Japan, China, Korea, India and Australia/New Zealand. The first two of these are complemented by FTAs concluded with individual ASEAN countries.[8] The EU might eventually do the same, although ASEAN countries and the EU have decided to first negotiate on an EU-to-ASEAN-country basis (Pelkmans and Mustilli 2013). This demonstration of ASEAN's de facto common trade policy is amazing and a clear proof of the pragmatism in ASEAN economic integration. The political will to have a joint but intergovernmental trade policy precisely with ASEAN's main trading partners in the region is readily explained outside the integration stages approach: it is of critical importance for ASEAN as a global (especially East Asian) 'production base'. It also shows that the distinction between FTAs and customs unions, so clear in GATT Article 24, has become less of an issue. Indeed, modern FTAs are quickly becoming 'deeper' and more 'comprehensive' as reflected in stages 3 and 4. What this means is that they already incorporate selective and conditional elements of 'higher' integration stages from the old classical approach (see Appendix) at the FTA stage. This is certainly also true for the few customs unions comparable to such deeper FTAs, the most prominent one being the EU–Turkey customs union of 1995, which comprises long harmonisation lists meant to

[8] See, e.g., Cremona *et al.* (2013); Inama and Sim (2013b); Kleimann (2013); Kuijper *et al.* (2013), all monographs from the project.

pre-empt or remove NTBs and a host of other provisions, rendering the intended final result more like a single market for goods. Basing the FTA/CU distinction on tariffs and (meanwhile forbidden in WTO) quotas is becoming less relevant in a world economy in which tariffs are low and declining even further.

Stage 3 is the 'FTA-plus', incorporating at least all the WTO obligations emanating from the many agreements (see notes for Table 2.1), as well as possibly some WTO-plus elements or deeper commitments. The 1994 WTO Agreements have long been a problem for AFTA and some issues are still not fully resolved in the ASEAN Trade in Goods Agreement (ATIGA), the consolidated goods agreement of ASEAN/AFTA.[9] At the time of the Bali Declaration on the AEC, no less than six WTO Agreements had not been incorporated (including pre-shipping inspection and customs valuation). This shows that the FTA-plus stage amounts to a considerable commitment over and above the classical FTA. On the other hand, the erstwhile WTO members of ASEAN were bound by these agreements anyway, which seems to point to some foot-dragging. One might define stage 3 for ASEAN as 'AFTA-plus', a minimalistic stage 3, with long transition times for some, and no WTO-plus elements at all. Yet the Bali Declaration announcing the AEC would seem to catapult ASEAN/AFTA to the far more ambitious, higher stages of Table 2.1, presumably even to stage 6 (single market). It is the apparent contradiction between declared market integration concepts and the actual market

[9] See Inama and Sim (2013a) for detail on the provisions and remaining problems of ATIGA.

access obligations implemented or entered into which justifies careful study of the economic and factual meaning of the integration concepts. Thus, several of the crucial points specified in the third column of stage 3 apply to ASEAN/AFTA as well. The GATS links under the ASEAN Framework Agreement on Services (AFAS) at the time of Bali and the almost complete failure to address technical barriers to trade (TBTs) and sanitary and phytosanitary (SPS) measures as barriers testify that AFTA-plus was at best a bare minimum of stage 3.

With stage 4 market integration moves decisively beyond the WTO. Table 2.1 specifies a range of policy domains, but we shall concentrate here on three of them: services; 'equivalence' as a way to avoid or reduce TBTs and SPS barriers; and positive integration. The liberalisation of services is a litmus test of stage 4. There are many sub-markets in services and most of them have traditionally been shielded from trade liberalisation. In fact, it is even worse: the liberalisation of services is, more often than not, interdependent with the liberalisation of factor movements. This is most obvious in financial markets: not only is the distinction between certain financial services and financial capital sometimes very difficult to make, it is also true that, when there are (financial) capital controls, intra-group cross-border financial services will often be severely hampered. The converse need not be correct: in the absence of capital controls, all kinds of restrictions – both domestic and cross-border – on financial services may be maintained. Another category where services and mobile factors are intertwined is found in temporary cross-border service provision, which (as mode 4, GATS indicates) is executed by mobile staff from the company (from another country in the region) that has won the service contract.

A third, and presumably more important, linkage is the direct local provision of services by a subsidiary of a company coming from elsewhere in the region (mode 3). Since the tradability of services is problematic in many cases – even when this is somewhat less the case than in the 1960s due to ICT – or even impossible, the common method of serving clients in the destination country is to opt for FDI. Such clients may well be multinationals, and service providers may be keen to keep up their long-term relationship with a major client, particularly when providers internationalise. The multinational, too, might wish to bring along trusted service providers with, say, FDI in goods. Therefore, in stages 4 and certainly 5 and 6, services are a central element. Preferably in stage 4, one should begin to address the interdependence between services and factor movements in such a way that service providers can employ the business model they prefer. It goes without saying that these considerations are crucial for ASEAN and the avowed aims of the AEC, which include, prominently, the attractiveness of the region for global FDI. More precisely, recent economic research has demonstrated that a range of services are critical to the smooth functioning of global value chains (see also section 4.3) – liberalisation of such services should be expected to render them more competitive, which is attractive for multinationals seeking ASEAN as a production base. At the same time, it can be regarded as one of the building blocks of the ASEAN single market, whatever its ultimate ambition.

'Equivalence' in technical aspects of risk regulation, including SPS, or (sometimes) services regulation, seems to be a lighter form of resolving the barriers arising from differences in regulatory regimes of countries than harmonisation or common regulation. At first sight, it suggests that practically no positive integration would be needed. Also, from an economic point of view, equivalence is appealing; it strongly suggests that what matters is the health, or safety or environmental objective, *not* the technical detail of achieving this objective. This idea accords well with the economic approach of market regulation, namely, what justifies regulation in markets is the market failure. A risk regulation objective is precisely the reduction of a safety or health risk to a tolerable level preferred by society, and this risk reduction removes the market failure – the technical detail does not matter for the end result and, hence, should not be a reason for country A or B to stop imports, only the failure to reach the *objective* should matter. Equivalence is based on this idea: if technical details are not identical, but the end result achieves the objective, there is no justification for blocking or hindering imports. But in actual practice, numerous instances inside the EU, let alone in the WTO, have shown that, without positive integration building trust, it has proven to be difficult to overcome TBT or SPS barriers on the basis of equivalence.[10] Many mutual recognition agreements (MRAs) have suffered the same fate, for example, that between the United States and the EU on medical devices, electrical safety and pharma. It means that stage 4 will entail a degree of positive integration in

[10] Documented in considerable detail in Pelkmans (2007) on mutual recognition inside the EU. Interestingly, although mutual recognition avoids EU regulation and relies on national regulation under constraints, the EU has overcome the perennial problems with mutual recognition by means of a (procedural) *EU regulation* on mutual recognition, forcing a shift in the burden of proof to the member states when firms expect treatment under mutual recognition (in goods). See Pelkmans (2012b).

committees of a quasi-regulatory nature or via prior regulatory consultation (prior to new regulation), agreements or conventions on mutual recognition, close cooperation in selective standard-setting or selective harmonisation.

What can be avoided or employed in a most minimalistic fashion in stage 3, can no longer be neglected or bypassed in stage 4 positive integration. As noted, barriers can be found at the border or 'behind the border'. The latter refers to discretion about or restrictions on (conduct of) non-local business incorporated in domestic regulation or arising from the powers of bodies that can control or condition market entry (from licensing to inspection, or network industry regulators, etc.). For short, we shall refer to all these as 'regulatory barriers'. Selectively, regulatory barriers might also be imposed at the border itself. The critical issue here is that it is *not* conceivable to enjoy a deep and comprehensive FTA as defined in stage 4 *merely* based on 'negative' integration. Insisting on mere negative integration would yield a *fragmented* market of the FTA partners, which would suffer from appreciable distortions as well. Dependent on degrees of national regulatory interventionism, one needs different, but in any event considerable, degrees of 'positive integration', as shown with risk regulation above. Such positive integration is not (usually) comparable to that of the EU, that is, it need neither – or only exceptionally – imply common regulation, nor common institutions with delegated powers. Nonetheless, weaker intergovernmental institutions – but with some power – and lighter regulatory solutions, including joint monitoring, joint standard setting, mutual acceptance of specific tests (e.g., in pharma or cosmetics), agreements on interoperability or compatibility, diploma recognition (a kind of equivalence) for specific professional service providers, reference to international conventions (e.g., the ILO core conventions) and arbitration (e.g., in investment disputes), exemplify such positive integration.

Stage 5 is the classical common market as invented by the Spaak committee – the founding fathers of the EEC Treaty – in 1956. It is characterised by free market access between the member states of the group in goods, services, labour and capital. This high stage of market integration is found only in federations such as the United States, Canada, Malaysia, Australia, India and Switzerland. The only group of *countries*, rather than a single federal country, that has introduced a common market is the EU in the Rome (EEC) Treaty of 1957.[11] The starting point consists of the fundamental market access freedoms in the four markets guaranteed in the treaty. Having those freedoms firmly and unequivocally written into the founding treaty, in turn, must imply several powerful mechanisms to ensure: (a) the development of the common market via numerous implementing measures over time; (b) that not too many and/or too important opt-outs or exceptions exist or persist; (c) that decision-making is not bogged down unnecessarily by endless veto practices, hence, qualified majority voting; and (d) that implementation, interpretation and enforcement is subject to independent judicial review on a routine basis, preceded by less costly, preemptive or cooperative approaches to solving such problems. Because most services, many goods and labour markets are regulated, a strong dose of ambitious positive integration is a

[11] Although variants of the concept have been adopted in Central America and in Caribbean market integration.

sine qua non in order for such deep market integration to have any chance of success. Without a body of common regulation and authoritative case law, it is unthinkable that a common market could be successfully established, let alone function properly. However, EU experience has revealed that even the Rome Treaty was not ambitious enough for a genuine common market to get off the ground: it allowed vetoes to continue (with dire consequences) and critical weaknesses in services, some goods markets and labour market regulation kept the practical achievements far below stage 5 until the mid-1980s.[12] The breakthrough of the first re-write of the Rome Treaty (the 1985 Single European Act) consisted precisely in removing the crippling veto system for most common market decisions, and in a sharper, more committing and functional definition of what the internal market (the new term for the common market in the Act) was meant to be.[13] Two options to further improve the common market and its functioning include a common anti-trust policy and some common funding for cross-border infrastructure and common adjustment support.

Stage 5 may eventually work and deliver a common market. Its pro-competitive effects should generate higher economic welfare, additional to that which member states on their

[12] The 'why and how' is analysed in Pelkmans (1985), and more politically in the Albert and Ball report (1983).

[13] See Ehlermann (1986) for an excellent account. It should be noted that the new approach to technical regulation and standards, inspired by mutual recognition, and what we now call 'better regulation' principles, also contributed to the swift deepening and widening of the common market. Moreover, in capital movements, the determination of the EU countries to lift lingering exchange controls (though not obligatory) also helped.

own could have generated. But this need not mean that it would amount to a 'single market'. In a way, the single market is an aspiration, not a legal or regulatory concept. Indeed, as an *economic* concept, it is more like an end result measured by economic indicators. Operationalising a single market is hard to do authoritatively, but undoubtedly it is more ambitious still than a common market in the sense of stage 5. Some specification, hinging on how economists see a single market, will be provided in section 3.3.2. 'Deepening' to a single market in the conceptual meaning of the stages approach is therefore extremely challenging. Even the EU, which accepts far-reaching positive integration routinely and more so with successive new treaties since its first re-write in 1985,[14] has not yet accomplished a genuine single market in the stages-approach meaning, with some elements (such as a common labour market) being still far off. For a good understanding, the EU has accomplished great advances in deeper market integration, and the dynamism in this respect has not yet petered out. This unique experiment demonstrates how incredibly ambitious a fully-fledged single market really is.

What the stages approach fails to provide is a clear-cut foundation for the AEC. But it helps to chart the possible substance of negative and perhaps positive market integration, whilst at least clarifying the broad options. Before going much deeper into the concrete aspects of the AEC, which is done later

[14] The Single European Act 1985, the Maastricht Treaty 1991 and the 2009 Lisbon Treaty are the three re-writes that have added substantially to the degree and intensity of positive integration. Further developments were witnessed during the recent sovereign debt crisis not just for the Eurozone only, but for the EU as a whole.

Box 2.1 What explains the moves to higher stages of market integration?

The logic of the stages approach, classic or modern, is that of a high building with many floors. One understands why a defined, more ambitious ('higher') stage follows defined lower stages. What remains unclear is why countries would wish to move up the stages to the higher or highest floors of the building. In a weaker form, the example has been set by the WTO. Whilst the GATT began with a pure tariff approach (and the OEEC in Europe dealt with quantitative restrictions and how to overcome them), after seven GATT Rounds (in 1995) a significant widening of scope in addressing barriers to trade and some deepening had taken place. The incentives behind this development consisted of the lowering of trade costs once the benefits of world trade in goods and services had been recognised more widely. The WTO hardly has positive integration, but it does entail credible dispute settlement with 'hard' principles and built-up case law. This is explained by the deepened market interdependence of trading partners seeking sufficient certainty for their transactions and, ultimately, for what they have invested in. In economic regionalism such mechanisms play an even more important role for the first three stages. Stage 3 of Table 2.1 is in fact a deeper and wider instance of what the WTO is nowadays. Moving beyond that stage 3 might still be regarded as an extension of the route that the front-runners in the WTO would prefer, as trade costs might be reduced by deeper integration

Box 2.1 (cont.)

(e.g., equivalence clauses, customs performance, public procurement), but it goes beyond WTO-plus in adopting obligations in, for example, competition policy and investment in a desire to enjoy still better market access and greater regulatory convergence (level playing field). This changes decisively with stages 5 and 6. The prior fundamental commitment of giving free market access in goods, services and factors of production becomes the linchpin of market integration. How far positive integration can reach depends not only on the initial negotiation position for, say, a treaty, but also on dynamic mechanisms building on the far-reaching and partly unforeseeable consequences of implementing both negative and positive integration in detail. If a functional approach is taken, as in the EU, the 'inner dynamics' of such long-term processes may hinge on spill-overs between different policy domains or logical extensions of earlier deepening. However, that is not automatic and the adjustments or unforeseen implications might prompt protest, or a call for differentiation, or policy reversals or at the limit even 'exit'. In Czechoslovakia in 1993, a dysfunctional political drive split the country into two polities, whilst keeping a customs union (with mostly common technical regulations) and a common labour market. Stage 6 (single market) can be reached only if an extraordinary consensus in the decision-making as well as irreversible legal disciplines by higher common courts coincide to eradicate systematically the

Box 2.1 (cont.)

lingering barriers or shortcomings in positive integration. In the EU, for example, the sensitivities have waned over time. Thus, instead of 'directives' with national implementation (allowing some differentiation as to local instruments or legal 'fit') nowadays many decisions on the still deepening internal market assume the form of an 'EU regulation', which has direct effects on economic agents (without even passing national parliaments). Such 'inner dynamics' can work as long as integration processes are broadly kept functional and the prior fundamental commitment of fully-fledged mutual market access remains essentially unquestioned.

in this book, one can say little more than that the AEC 'vision' might seem to aspire to reach stage 4, if not beyond.

But 'beyond', and in particular a 'single market' (stage 6), amounts to the most demanding of all efforts towards market integration, which seems puzzling and hardly credible. Aspiring to achieve a 'single' market while ASEAN is allergic to the slightest form of centralisation and/or to 'hard' enforcement overruling the autonomy ('sovereignty') of its Member States or, indeed, more generally to 'positive integration', sounds at the very least 'incoherent' against the background of the modern integration stages approach. Moreover, ASEAN could not logically maintain its FTA status in a single or even common market. Even for stage 4, can ASEAN maintain its AFTA (not having convergent tariffs and insisting on national trade policies) in its classical form, causing fragmentation, even when, in the removal of technical barriers, services, intellectual property rights (IPRs), investment and some other areas, ambition has increased far beyond the classical FTA stage?[15] In short, the modern stages approach demonstrates that ASEAN will face stark choices in making an AEC that is living up to the aspirations of the Bali 'vision' work.

2.3 Why credibility and transparency matter

Whereas the economic rationale of economic integration consists of the net benefits of 'economic welfare' for society as a whole, the effectiveness of an economic integration model and its detailed implementation and execution hinges on the *actually induced* responses of economic agents to the opportunities inherent in cross-border liberalisation and convergent regulation, harmonisation and/or mutual recognition. Most of the time the critical economic agents responding to opportunities created by an AEC will be in business, including investors. Sometimes, consumers or their associations may gear into action as well via cross-border shopping or delegated trading.

Elegantly drafted government or ASEAN communiqués or press releases are not compelling in and by themselves. Between them, negotiators or national civil

[15] See also Thio and Venzke (2013), addressing the internal effects of ASEAN concluding external trade and investment agreements from a legal point of view.

servants may consider their consensual compromises on the building blocks of the AEC as commendable achievements. However, what matters for economic benefits is *how markets see it*. This is not to say that markets are always 'right' or that, at times, they might not be slow to exploit regional integration opportunities because it might require new business models. But, sooner or later, some entrepreneurs will test new rules or newly attained freedoms. And that is how it should be. As noted, their actual responses, induced by AEC-driven opportunities, is what enables fiercer competition, new entry, restructuring, new ideas, new business models, more economies of scale and scope, greater variety and choice, better integration in global value chains and, in many cases, lower prices. Business will only act, however, when the building blocks of the AEC are credible to them. Credibility is hard to define in general, but is determined by a range of factors that can be identified.

Credibility of 'deeper' economic integration is, first of all, determined by some of the fundamentals (see section 2.1), such as the political framework, the nature of the long-term commitments of the participating countries and the propensity of the group to opt for partial or selective integration. Admittedly, these aspects are impossible to measure objectively, but business is capable of 'reading' the fundamentals in a more pragmatic fashion and will get better at it over time. Given that these fundamentals matter for credibility, this issue goes to the heart of the ambition of ASEAN's integration strategy. In the last twenty-five years, ASEAN has moved on each one of these three fundamentals. Its political framework has been firmed somewhat in that ministerial and senior officials' meetings have become more operational due to the functional requirements of AFTA and AFTA-plus. The credibility of AFTA for business has almost certainly improved, albeit after many years, with more suitable criteria for origin rules, a harmonised tariff nomenclature and attempts to lower transaction costs for customs clearing. This can be extended to AEC-building, prompted by accepted tools such as the Roadmap and scorecards. The minimum long-term commitment of ASEAN Member States has, at long last, been codified in the ASEAN Charter. And the very idea of an AEC has stimulated the emergence of a more holistic concept of 'deeper' economic integration, which envelops several isolated initiatives (e.g., the AFAS on services and the ASEAN Investment Area on investment), thereby probably reducing the strong inclination to opt for selectivity.

A second determinant of credibility is found in the degree of discipline imposed on the discretion of ASEAN Member States to intervene or regulate domestically in policy domains under AFTA or AEC rules and obligations. As a highly decentralised, intergovernmental system, with Member States remaining very sensitive to any (perceived or real) instance of centralisation, it is critical how AEC-type obligations are actually complied with at the national level. Amongst ASEAN scholars and in business circles, there is quite some scepticism whether ASEAN can ensure the compliance of its Member States.[16] Often, the comparison is made with the EU

[16] See the project papers by Dehousse and Aziz (2013); Quah *et al.* (2013); Sim and Inama (2013a); Weiler (2013). See also Beckman *et al.* (2013).

having extensive and strict implementation and enforcement powers.[17] However, this comparison makes no sense because the EU is not a model that ASEAN wants to strive after. But there is an alternative option exemplified by a group which is equally decentralised and is similarly sensitive to centralisation: NAFTA.[18] NAFTA is a modern, upgraded FTA-plus, with a considerable overlap in substance with what the AEC probably stands for (see Chapter 5). Implementation and compliance is perhaps not perfect (e.g., in anti-dumping there have been some problems; dispute settlement leaves something to be desired), but overall is regarded as satisfactory and credible by business. Simplifying here, proper implementation and credible enforcement and compliance is essentially achieved in two ways: one is having a very detailed (NAFTA) treaty at the outset of close to 2,000 pages (with annexes); the other is the powerful private litigation culture driven by damage compensation. In contrast, ASEAN typically wants political leaders to express a vision first and work out, step by step, the details and implications later, always under the tight control of national governments. This approach is the very opposite of the NAFTA one. It creates uncertainty with business and forces companies interested in the ASEAN market as a whole into a 'waiting attitude' for many years, which they thoroughly dislike or, more importantly,

17 For an extensive overview of today's implementation and enforcement mechanisms of the EU's single market, both in terms of 'hard' law and by means of 'preventive' and 'cooperative' (between the European Commission and Member States) mechanisms, including detailed empirical analysis, see Pelkmans and Correia de Brito (2012).

18 If not more so, because they do not even have a central secretariat supporting negotiations and initiatives.

cannot afford given the competitive pressures under globalisation. For multinationals and far-sighted ASEAN companies, such an approach pre-empts strategy. Once building blocks are agreed at ASEAN ministerial level, the implementation and enforcement or compliance mechanisms are not disciplined in any serious way, neither by EU-type powers (soft or hard) nor by effective private litigation against national governments failing to live up to AEC obligations. All that ASEAN offers is a weak dispute settlement mechanism, the panel reports of which end up in the intergovernmental machinery of ASEAN, which might or might not accommodate the conclusion. Even the monitoring of national implementation seems to be a problem.[19]

Moreover, there is no ASEAN or AEC court, and, failing litigation in national courts, there is no authoritative interpretation of 'ASEAN law' which would serve all, but especially business. The scorecards, employed to follow national implementation of the Roadmap decisions, are not public; only the overall scores are. But even if they were, one wonders to what extent this would satisfy the quest of businesses for legal certainty. Here the EU has taught a lesson which is independent of its 'model' and therefore of relevance to ASEAN as well. EU member states often implement in ways that do not fully reflect the letter and spirit of EU-level decisions – this was true four decades ago and it remains a fact today, albeit less so. The Commission spends considerable resources on guiding and enforcing proper national implementation, not to mention the CJEU which deals with many unresolved

[19] See Chesterman and Yusuf (2013)

instances year after year.[20] These hard facts become even more striking once one realises that: (a) the EU countries do accept centralisation far more than ASEAN; (b) national administrations all have specialists in EU law; (c) there is extensive annual reporting on the quality of implementation, including 'naming and shaming'; and (d) in numerous cases, it is possible for business or citizens to sue member states in national courts (for wrong implementation) for damages. In this light, one can harbour no illusions about what ASEAN Member States' implementation records are or will be in future, given that none of the four (analogous) conditions, which greatly help the EU system to remain credible, prevail in ASEAN. The multi-annual cumulation of half-baked or 'wrong' implementation in ten ASEAN countries of numerous AEC-driven rules and other details and/or forms of liberalisation is bound to seriously threaten the credibility of the AEC in markets. We repeat: effective implementation and enforcement is merely an expression of what ASEAN Member States have commonly and voluntarily agreed, it does *not* require any form of 'centralisation' or supranationalism, as NAFTA has shown so clearly. The national follow-up of common decisions and the acceptance of its legal consequences are part and parcel of these decisions. ASEAN Member States should not act as if ASEAN is not 'them'. Precisely because there is not the slightest centralisation, every ASEAN decision is a consensual decision of all Member States. Credibility is a direct function of the

[20] For detailed empirics, see Pelkmans and Correia de Brito (2012).

willingness and capacity to live up to one's own national decisions in the ASEAN context.

Another important point is transparency. *Transparency* gives confidence and a degree of predictability (in particular, in combination with credibility), the lack of transparency breeds suspicion and makes uncertainty linger. Transparency is needed for business planning and certainty for investors. One may also regard transparency as a fundamental right of citizens in democracies, as a necessity for the rule of law and as a basis for sound contractual relations. All these remarks are nothing new, of course. Yet transparency remains a concern in ASEAN. One can understand the desire for less transparency in sensitive political diplomacy, but there is simply no case for reduced transparency when building up the AEC. As noted, the actually induced business decisions will eventually cause the AEC to work as intended, and a lack of transparency does not inspire much confidence in the process. One can applaud the much greater clarity about ASEAN and AFTA due to the ASEAN Secretariat's rich website and greater publicity in general – something that was badly lacking in the early 1990s. But in the AEC, ASEAN will need to become fully open as a routine, day after day. Detail and specificity as well as the results of monitoring of implementation matter for business to make their plans operational. Since the ASEAN Charter of 2007 has been adopted, ASEAN has because more open to these kinds of discussions. Thus, the ASEAN 2014 Summit of May 2014 in Nay Pyi Taw, in the Declaration on the realisation of the AEC, emphasises in item 2 'to further enhance ASEAN cooperation in promoting democracy, good governance and the rule of law ... further enhance a rule based community of shared values and norms'. Transparency and credibility (e.g. of measures and regulations) are part and parcel of this perspective.

2.4 Strategic choices about AEC design

Building the AEC brick by brick need not be a problem, just like building a house, once the architectural design, the technical drawings and the craftsmanship of the workers have been taken care of. The focus here will be on *design* as a *strategic* issue for the coherence and effectiveness of the AEC. The question of the substance (the 'technical drawings' so to speak) and some details about specific aspects (the 'craftsmanship', so to speak) will be set out in Chapters 3 and 4.

We shall attempt to clarify the strategic choices ASEAN faces, for the AEC to be coherent and credible. We do this by asking four 'architectural' questions and compare the AEC with NAFTA, a credible and functioning FTA-plus with some similarities to what ASEAN presumably wants. The EU will be mentioned as well (only the bare essentials), but merely as a matter of contrast, that is, for the purpose of showing alternative answers to the four strategic choices. ASEAN, whether it likes it or not, cannot avoid these strategic choices. The advantage of a comparison with NAFTA and the EU is that both have coherent (though radically different) strategies, and the choices that underlie NAFTA should be interesting for the AEC. Should ASEAN decide not to opt for either, it would need to come up with a coherent approach itself, short of building an ill-functioning construct. The comparison with NAFTA here is solely about design. Once the substance of the AEC has been addressed in detail (in Chapters 3 and 4), the AEC, NAFTA and the EU will be compared on substance as well (in Chapter 5).[21]

For AEC architects to understand NAFTA's design one has to reflect on four closely linked strategic choices:

- What is the desired nature of economic regionalism?
- The degree of specificity and detail at the outset.
- The system of implementation, compliance and enforcement.
- Room and incentives for deepening and widening (of scope).

2.4.1 Strategic choice No. 1

NAFTA is a modern FTA-plus, incorporating generously WTO-based principles of trade law, aligning itself to (what has meanwhile become, after NAFTA was signed, a series of) separate GATT agreements from the Uruguay Round, often with additional features or disciplines.

This strategic choice must imply that NAFTA

- is intergovernmental;
- needs no more than a lean technical secretariat, solely tasked with information and basic organisational duties, but not with any coordination or agenda setting, let alone proposals;
- needs no common budget (other than for the small secretariat);

[21] The present subsection, as well as Chapter 5, has been inspired by Hew *et al.* (2004). However, the current text is updated and considerably revised (and shortened).

- is treaty-based (if only for Article 24 of GATT), with intrusive consequences for domestic regulatory discretion.

The first three of these four implications also apply to ASEAN/AEC. The fourth does not, although the post-Charter situation reduces uncertainty about what is 'binding' and what is not.

This strategic choice leaves some discretion as to *how far* one wishes to introduce elements of minimum regulatory provisions ('harmonisation') in certain areas so as to facilitate either trade in goods or services, as well as cross-border acquisitions or greenfield investments. The presumption is that such elements will be relatively few and unambitious. It would be inconsistent, on the one hand, to refuse to have a customs union with a common external tariff (and perhaps a common trade policy) as being too intrusive or constraining for national policy autonomy, while, on the other hand, embarking upon difficult programmes of harmonisation in a comprehensive FTA-plus inspired by WTO-type principles, but little more than that. WTO and other intergovernmental cooperation typically avoids harmonisation except where indispensable. At the same time, one should not fail to notice that the many GATT agreements (dated later than NAFTA, but inspired by it) do incorporate some modest forms of minimum provisions that have the great advantage of rooting out the worst instances of discrimination in trade and investment.

2.4.2 *Strategic choice No. 2*

NAFTA has clearly opted for a high degree of specificity and detail in the treaty *from the outset*, rather than relying on a process of gradual refinement following the ratification of a framework treaty. Not only has the NAFTA treaty specified a large number of positive obligations (disciplines and rights) for the member states or their economic agents, it has routinely added many instances of negative obligations (i.e., what member states are prohibited from doing, e.g., to evade the positive obligations) that provide extra assurances and clarity for business. The fundamental choice for assuring unambiguous rights and obligations in a regional treaty of this kind is that between the *transfer of decision-making powers* to a central level which is to deliver the specification in an effective manner, and *far-reaching* positive and negative *specification from the outset* (thereby presumably obviating any form of delegation of decision-making to a central organ). Anything in between tends to lead to much greater uncertainty (also for business) and a much longer process of 'building-up'.

ASEAN has, so far, refused to go for either option. Instead, it opted for a somewhat open-ended idea in the Bali Summit Declaration, which has gradually been elaborated in the twelve-year period up to 2015 inclusive. Not only is this a long road of discovery, the process – consensus-based as it is – risks being slower than initially desired and with plenty of compromises given the highly decentralised decision-making dispersed over many policy domains. NAFTA has made an unambiguous choice in favour of the second approach: far-reaching specification of positive and negative obligations and rights in many horizontal and sectoral domains. In the presence of a well-functioning legal system, this generates strong incentives for compliance, since otherwise private litigation will take over. Moreover, business actors can act based on the predictability of the liberalisation that is forthcoming. In opting for the method of detailed specification, NAFTA could afford to decline any transfer of power to a central level.

2.4.3 *Strategic choice No. 3*

How to deal with implementation, compliance and enforcement? It is important for AEC architects to appreciate that the institutional and legal issues are not the whole story in the NAFTA case. The United States has a tradition of trade remedy laws and practices (such as countervailing duties and anti-dumping), as well as safeguards (e.g., in textiles and steel), which exposed the weaknesses of its multilateral commitments. Given that Canada was already the largest trading partner of the United States, and that Mexico's potential was perhaps even greater in this respect, not just free trade, but indeed *assured* market access was critical to the United States' neighbours. Therefore, the choices for implementation, compliance and enforcement were not only determined by the regular treaty obligations themselves – again, quite detailed – but first of all by the credibility of the treaty provisions in limiting US discretion to resort to safeguards or to escape clauses in a unilateral fashion. Both Canada and Mexico were willing to go quite far in order to 'lock in' the United States (and the US Congress).

Thus, the agreed dispute settlement had to satisfy two conditions: (1) binding the United States (not least the US Congress with its constitutional trade powers); and (2) offering least-cost, effective dispute settlement that would be so attractive that costly and discouraging private litigation (and the enormous interests of the law firms) would only serve as a last resort or in extreme cases. NAFTA accomplished this, a major benefit for Mexico and Canada, and even for the general interest of the United States.

However, one should not fail to notice the underlying assumption here. The United States has to stick to its commitment and accept both the letter and the spirit of the dispute settlement. Broadly speaking, the United States has done this, helped by accommodation of the more protectionist sectors in the treaty (clothing and cars) and by exceptions (e.g., airlines), taking the expected pressures off the dispute settlement system.[22] Even so, given the restrictive anti-dumping practices of the United States, dispute settlement has been disappointing in this domain since the minimal discretion (e.g., appointing panel members) has been exploited to frustrate the process.

The lessons for ASEAN should therefore be sought in the methods and detail of dispute settlement, as well as in the stringent domestic legal and institutional requirements of compliance (removing or amending domestic laws conflicting with the treaty), and of private litigation as a last resort (for matters of interpretation or enforcement). The incentives in ASEAN are not entirely comparable with the NAFTA case. However, the credibility of ASEAN for multinational business is just as critical as in NAFTA or indeed in any form of deeper economic regionalism.

[22] For example, textiles and clothing are protected by strict origin rules, for example, a high (NAFTA) origin percentage for yarn and cloth before clothing enjoys preferences; similar provisions apply to cars. See also the detailed substantive comparison table in Chapter 5, Table 5.1.

What NAFTA brings out forcefully is that business and others who take risks and invest their own money, or indeed borrow capital, should feel assured that the system is credible. Multinationals do business worldwide and they will hesitate to invest or compete if that assurance is not available. In East Asia, surely, they can go elsewhere. Like NAFTA, the AEC would have to deliver. At the moment, it does not, by any means, as will be shown later.

2.4.4 *Strategic choice No. 4*

Should one build into the treaty both incentives and decision-making in order to generate *further dynamics* of deepening and widening? NAFTA has not done this. The treaty is the end result. Indeed, this is the same for ASEAN: the AEC has been declared the end goal. The difference remaining is obviously that the AEC is not well defined, whereas NAFTA was precisely defined right from the beginning. It would not be surprising if the AEC were to deepen and widen over time, once the full consequences of market integration logic begin to sink in. Careful reading of the AEC Roadmap and subsequent proposals already shows some such dynamics (see section 3.4).

On these four strategic choices, the AEC and NAFTA are more alike than is often held to be the case. On the first choice, the similarities are striking, except for the treaty. However, the recent evolution in ASEAN (e.g., with the Charter and new agreements) would seem to be moving in a more legal direction due to the requirements of deeper market integration and the ASEAN experiences with FTAs with third countries. On the second choice (specificity and detail at the outset), NAFTA and ASEAN have opted for radically different approaches. However, now that ASEAN has proven capable of setting the AEC process in motion and elaborating it all the time, the possibility becomes more real that, over time, the difference will narrow considerably. On the third choice (implementation, compliance and enforcement), the extreme assurances so critical to NAFTA partners do not play a role in the AEC. Still, there is no denying that ASEAN credibility suffers, given the incapacity of the group to deliver a credible and routinely working system of assuring implementation and enforcement, let alone a dispute settlement procedure which is actually used.[23] Curiously, some selective dispute settlement (in fact, arbitration) with respect to investment protection has already been accepted. This might help to overcome this 'taboo' in the near future. Once it is in place, the more important implementation questions have to be addressed seriously. The NAFTA logic makes sense. Since the EU approach of 'supreme' EU law is no alternative, ASEAN should come up with another approach or consider a solid variant of the NAFTA approach. On the fourth choice (no future dynamics), again, the AEC and NAFTA concur.

2.5 Economic rationale of the AEC

The AEC has not been inaugurated on the basis of a thorough economic impact assessment or a profound study by, say, an economic research consortium or the Asian Development Bank (ADB). The leaders of ASEAN have commissioned an

[23] For extensive detail, see Mayer *et al.* (2013); Inama and Sim (2013a).

interesting study from McKinsey (2003) using a blend of detailed descriptive analysis of barriers inside and weaknesses of ASEAN/AFTA, with practical surveys from ASEAN and multinational business. The study contextualises the East Asian competition for world class investors, with considerable attention given to the future significance of China. McKinsey touched upon aspects little discussed in AFTA circles up until 2003, yet crucial for business and value chains, such as technical standards and technical barriers, while being much more plain and open than usual with respect to topics such as the corruption and red tape in customs or the lack of transparency in authorising or not direct investment.[24] It was probably the first time that practical business experiences in many ASEAN countries were tabled systematically, via the 'safe' route of this report. The report is likely to have stimulated the leaders to issue the Bali Declaration, but unfortunately little more.

So far, ASEAN has never articulated the economic rationale(s) of the AEC in a careful study exploring various options driven by what economic analysis might suggest. Of course, in the present conceptual study we cannot pretend to fill this gap in a few pages. Nevertheless, an 'economic' community is exceedingly hard to conceptualise if one does not move beyond some nebulous generalities about the underlying economic rationale(s). Therefore, we offer a reflection on two different, though partly overlapping, economic 'rationales' of the AEC:

[24] Unfortunately, the McKinsey study was not published, another example of a counterproductive prudency on the part of ASEAN leaders, at least if they wish to realise an ambitious undertaking such as the AEC.

Box 2.2 Can economic theory underpin the ASEAN Economic Community ?

In its classical form, the economic theory of regionalism has great difficulty in providing rational economic arguments in favour of free trade areas and customs unions. The received wisdom is that multilateral liberalisation is always better, unless the group has enough economic power in world trade to force a beneficial shift in its terms-of-trade (at the expense of other countries in the world). It is most unlikely that ASEAN had any such economic power when AFTA was initiated, and that is probably still valid today now that the AEC is being built up. The suggestion once made by Johnson (1965) and Cooper and Massell (1965) is that developing countries, having a strong preference for promoting industrialisation, could exploit regionalism to boost industrial goods exports to each other. However, this would only work well if specialisation in industrial goods would be sufficiently different between the group's countries. It would also require high enough protection vis-à-vis OECD countries, which might well turn out to be costly in the longer run by failing to allow dynamic market adjustments, hence, becoming less, not more, competitive over time. However, the fact is that AFTA was much more used by ASEAN countries as an experiment (a stepping stone, perhaps) anticipating worldwide liberalisation in the Uruguay Round and later. In other words, Cooper/Massell/Johnson-type of joint protection is the opposite of what AFTA did:

Box 2.2 (cont.)

together with the gradual intra-AFTA reduction of tariffs, ASEAN countries all lowered external MFN tariffs as well as external applied tariffs.

A combination of two critical economic motives would seem to explain ASEAN's decision to raise its ambition and go for the AEC as a much more wide-ranging and deeper form of economic regionalism. The first is that economic openness and especially market access for industrial goods is critical for (greater) participation in global value chains, seen as a crucial leverage to increase economic growth via trade. Global value chains (GVCs) have no place in classical trade theory, hence, the lack of 'fit'. GVCs do not necessitate economic regionalism, but ASEAN thinking (and some of its earlier practices of 'industrial complementation') is strongly influenced by the Japanese 'flying geese' model, with the highly differentiated comparative advantages inside ASEAN allowing both intra-ASEAN as well as external exploitation. The second and closely related motive is about foreign direct investment. GVCs are about both trade and FDI. The analytical literature began to incorporate this trade and investment nexus into theory in the late 1990s (e.g., Ethier 1998) but it has been adopted with more gusto in the policy literature on economic regionalism (e.g., Bergsten 1995; Whalley 1996; Pelkmans and Brenton 1998). There is no doubt that both motives play a powerful role in ASEAN and its AEC decision in 2003 and even more so today. However, there is a dynamic element which further

Box 2.2 (cont.)

strengthens this reasoning: commitment to sound economic policies. North/South regionalism was already regarded as a form of 'commitment', that is, a firm signal of going for sound economic reforms and avoiding 'policy reversals'. Such commitments are improving the investment climate and make a North/South agreement far more attractive. ASEAN initially had no obvious North/South FTA to consider and hence needed to come up with a long-term strategy to credibly improve commitment to sound economic policymaking, in turn, improving the investment climate and the attraction for GVCs in the region. The AEC can be interpreted as such a long-term strategy, in sharp contrast to ASEAN's earlier practice of weak and ad-hoc 'cooperation' without any degree of binding. This perspective helps to explain its emphasis on both the 'single market' idea and its 'production base'. Equally, it is consistent with a simultaneous internal and (liberalising) external FTA strategy practiced by ASEAN since the early 2000s.

(1) *A cooperative ASEAN-led development strategy*, complementing national variants of 'open economies' development strategies of ASEAN countries, exploiting the possibilities of distinct levels of development in ASEAN and stimulating a catch-up approach inspired by the 'flying geese' pattern. This is about rendering ASEAN as a region attractive for investment at all levels of development, while facilitating the intra-ASEAN linkages that affiliates of multinationals might wish to exploit.

(2) *A pro-competitive quasi-single market strategy for development*, combining far-reaching negative and at least the necessary positive market integration in order to overcome or pre-empt market failures at the ASEAN level, complemented by intergovernmental economic cooperation and emulation of 'best practices' at national level.

2.5.1 *A cooperative ASEAN-led growth development strategy*

During the last few decades ASEAN countries have gradually switched to more market-driven economic policies, together with a steady opening up of their economies to one another as well as to the world. Since early 2013, all ten ASEAN countries have become WTO contracting parties. AFTA, as well as the steady lowering of MFN tariffs (both bound and applied), are important manifestations of this trend. The recent series of individual and common FTAs concluded or under negotiations have accentuated the opening up. Domestically, ASEAN countries have reformed and market incentives play a much more important role than, say, when AFTA was initiated in 1992. Before and shortly after the East Asian financial crisis, ASEAN countries have grown quite healthily (between 2000 and 2007, some 7 per cent annually for Indonesia on average and around 5 per cent for ASEAN-5), with more recent economic growth seemingly little affected by the worldwide economic crisis. Catch-up growth of the poor and the lower middle income countries of ASEAN has been impressive during the last five years despite the global slowdown. Table 2.2 documents this trend and the expectation that it will continue.

Table 2.2 *Real annual GDP growth rates of ASEAN countries, 2008–14 (%)*

	2008	2009	2010	2011	2012	2013*	2014*
Brunei D.	−1.9	−1.8	2.6	2.2	1.0	1.8	2.0
Cambodia	6.7	0.1	6.0	7.1	7.2	7.2	7.5
Indonesia	6.0	4.6	6.2	6.5	6.2	6.4	6.6
Lao PDR	7.2	7.3	7.5	7.8	7.9	7.7	7.7
Malaysia	4.8	−1.5	7.2	5.1	5.6	5.3	5.5
Myanmar	3.6	5.1	5.3	5.5	6.3	6.5	6.7
Philippines	4.2	1.1	7.6	3.9	6.6	6.0	5.9
Singapore	1.7	−0.8	14.8	5.2	1.3	2.6	3.7
Thailand	2.5	−2.3	7.8	0.1	6.4	4.9	5.0
Vietnam	6.3	5.3	6.8	5.9	5.0	5.2	5.6

Source: ADB, *Asian Development Outlook*, 2013, April, Appendix.
* forecasts.

One has to be careful in interpreting these secular growth rates for individual ASEAN countries, because the growth drivers – other than more market and less interventionism and less protectionism – vary from export of resources, or an emphasis on service exports in some countries, to a heavy emphasis on segments of global manufacturing value chains and plain exploitation of low wage/low skills/low tech comparative advantages in world trade. Moreover, with higher per capita incomes, domestic demand can become an important driver, too. Nevertheless, there is one secular characteristic in ASEAN economic growth: increasing trade and investment openness. Thus, (goods) trade to (nominal) GDP ratios for ASEAN-10 rose from 89 per cent in 1990 to 131 per cent in 2000, reducing to 107 per cent due to the global crisis in 2008, and since rising again to 116 per cent (2011). Conspicuous is the steep rise in this ratio for Cambodia, Myanmar, Lao and Vietnam (CMLV) and Brunei from 75 per cent in 1990, via 84 per cent in 2000, to 131 per cent in 2011. One also observes a steady rise in FDI from an annual average of US$35 billion in 1985–9, via an average of US$75 billion in 1995–9, to US$113 billion in the period 2000–6.[25]

ERIA (2012: vi) notes that ASEAN FDI inflows increased further, with no less than 75 per cent in the years 2007–2011. These trade and FDI characteristics convey the outward-oriented development strategies of ASEAN countries. It is crucial to add that this openness is largely with East Asia, the United States and the EU, much less with ASEAN itself. The ratio of intra-ASEAN goods trade to ASEAN's world trade (including ASEAN) long hovered around 25 per cent and has only moved up a little despite AFTA. It is mainly these stylised facts which are likely to have played a major role in the thinking behind the Bali Declaration.

Economic policy thinking in ASEAN countries (with the possible exception of Singapore and Brunei) is dominated by long-term development aspirations. Given the distinct levels of development in ASEAN, this translates into somewhat different strategies concerning inward FDI and trade. The interesting point is that this strategic differentiation can be accommodated in a single overarching strategy for the whole of ASEAN. The

[25] *Source*: Albada, Yap and Petri (2009: 84). Note these are flows over the balance of payments, a poor way of registering FDI. Stocks may also grow due to reinvested earnings and borrowing for, e.g., new plants. The source of the trade/GDP ratios is ADB Calculations (2012). Note that two countries also enjoy strong export growth in services: Singapore and the Philippines (the latter via explosive growth in world call centres).

inspiration is the old Japanese 'flying geese' model of a gradual shift of segments of industrial activity from countries losing comparative advantage (say, in labour-intensive and low-tech parts of production) to countries (in East Asia) still enjoying such comparative advantage, thereby accelerating their economic development. Once more developed, the latter countries might move up the value-added ladder of industrial and services development, and witness a renewed shift to countries prepared to open up but still having much lower wages. Initially, this might work for stand-alone subsidiaries in, say, textiles and clothing,[26] shoes and sporting goods, but later assembly operations might emerge in, say, export processing zones and so-called 'growth triangles' with complementing facilities or capabilities. Such assembly operations might be (and often have been) the beginning of capacity and skills development, especially once so-called backward and forward linkages to local suppliers and business-to-business (B2B) procurement grow in intensity and scope. Such greater sophistication and multiplier effects can, of course, be influenced by accompanying local policies.

The ASEAN region is highly diversified from very high income countries all the way to very poor countries. ASEAN is big, with its 550 million people and a relatively young population needing jobs. There is thus ample scope for the geese flying inside ASEAN. The AEC can be regarded as a strategic answer to this opportunity. Of course, the strategic

[26] One example: Cambodia has recently enjoyed a high growth rate, partly due to extreme specialisation in clothing exports (some 75 per cent of all goods exports).

answer was prompted by much greater urgency given the phenomenal rise of China. China is not only successful, but so large that it seemed capable of sucking in almost all FDI for assembly,[27] and possibly other segments of value chains, at the expense of countries such as those in ASEAN potentially or actually competing fiercely with China. Making the geese fly inside or towards ASEAN instead required a strategic shift, rendering FDI in the region much more attractive and offering an effective alternative or that assuring parts of value chains linked to the Chinese final assembly (in turn, often exported to the rest of the world). Indeed, in electronics – a sector where global value chains have invested in ASEAN countries such as Malaysia and the Philippines – mass-produced intermediate electronic goods move to China for final goods assembly. For the ASEAN countries that have already reached middle-income status, the desire is to ensure that new FDI is related to more sophisticated 'higher' segments of the value chain for which the economy has to avail of the skills, absorbed technology, specialised services, better logistics (again, lowering trade costs), and a technology and mobility infrastructure that can support this higher value-added generation, in turn supporting the continuation of a high growth strategy. For the medium developed ASEAN countries, it is critical to be able to capture new segments of the global value chains and/or somehow ensure, or at least stimulate, continuous upgrading of existing facilities, because getting 'stuck' with relatively low value-added segments of

[27] In 2010 some 43 per cent of Chinese exports still came from export processing zones. Source: WTO/JETRO (2010).

value chains will only lead to additional growth via greater volume effects (e.g., dependence on China and/or the OECD countries for more demand). It will fail to generate higher value-added per unit of exports, a crucial ingredient of catch-up growth with developed economies. And it creates vulnerabilities in, say, a global crisis when such demand drops dramatically.[28]

It is therefore worthwhile making a brief excursion to the empirical economics of global value chains. More strategically, it is also interesting to recall the recent attention to what is called 'the middle income trap', the apparent inability of medium income countries to develop and exploit their dynamic comparative advantages in ways that will allow them to become developed economies (as, e.g., Singapore and Korea have so successfully done). If they are at risk of getting stuck in the middle income trap, is the AEC an appropriate means to escape from it and move up faster?

The enormous attention to global value chains has not been reflected in a similar avalanche of solid economic work on the subject. It is only very recently that economic research has deepened and become more directly policy relevant. One reason is the sudden rise of Chinese participation since the mid-1990s. Another reason is the rapid spread and greater sophistication of the fragmentation of tasks over ever more complex value chains covering several, if not many,

[28] In Table 2.2 one observes precisely that in Malaysia, the Philippines and Thailand when in 2009 they experienced a sudden drop in growth as demand from China and ultimately OECD markets fell significantly (Cambodia, too, but this was due to domestic turbulence).

countries. This is particularly true in electronics, but to a considerable extent as well in automotive products or machine tools, and even in some toys, sports goods and specialty chemicals. Value chains have simply become much more important for both developing and developed countries. A third reason is the increasing concern of economists and policymakers alike that trade statistics no longer reflect what matters 'on the ground'. With the fragmentation of 'tasks' spread over many countries, goods move regularly over frontiers and their full invoice value is incorporated in trade statistics. With, for example, China becoming so important in assembly operations, what matters is to know the value-added part of the invoice at the frontier. In China, this is often rather low, which must imply that there is a lot of double counting. Thus, WTO/JETRO (2010: 104) found that counting solely value-added in China (the rest is imported value-added already incorporated in the intermediate good when entering China for assembly), the US 2005 deficit in goods trade with China would more than halve from US$218 billion to US$101 billion. Similarly, the US deficit in iPhones imported from China seems gigantic since the phones are assembled in China, yet the Chinese value-added share amounts only to 4 per cent, as other countries have contributed much more to the incorporated value-added (the United States itself, but, e.g., also Japan with 35 per cent).[29] New work by UNCTAD (2013)

[29] The reader may wonder why such issues were not addressed earlier in economics. The reason is that this requires first an alignment of detailed input–output statistics with trade statistics (with different classifications) which is complex, and subsequently extremely laborious matching exercises.

found that, for 2010, about US$5 trillion of world trade in goods (of US$19 trillion), or 28 per cent, is double-counted due to movements of intermediates in and out of countries. For ASEAN what matters is the development strategy and, hence, local value-added is the variable that matters. The development dimension of GVCs can be critical as UNCTAD (2013) has demonstrated, whereas the value-added trade of OECD countries is around 18 per cent of GDP this is no less than 30 per cent for developing countries. UNCTAD also found a positive correlation between country participation in GVCs and growth rates of GDP per capita, suggesting strong opportunities for longer-term industrial upgrading.

The ASEAN development strategy should be able to facilitate the attraction of FDI generating the more value-added in the chains the higher the level of development. It should also watch out for excessive dependencies on, for example, China and/or the ultimate markets for those final products, the OECD countries most of the time. Athukorala (2010) shows that the intensification of what is often called East Asian economic integration via these networks has not decreased the ultimate dependence on OECD markets; quite the contrary, it has further increased these linkages. In fact, the rapid growth of intra-East Asian goods trade is entirely due to intermediates, not final goods. But he also concludes that the China factor has not been a zero-sum game with, for example, ASEAN. Rather, it has added further dynamism in other East Asian countries. The question is, of course, what might happen once China begins to move up the value chain itself. Recent OECD work based on the new trade-compatible world input–output tables made for estimating more accurately value-added flows, shows that China is moving up the value chains rapidly, measured by export specialisation over many sectors and export quality based on unit values (De Backer 2011). In the East Asian context, this is likely to mean that simple assembly may well begin to be shifted to low income countries including CMLV. In clothing, this has already happened. For medium income ASEAN countries, it becomes ever more crucial to acquire FDI which is 'capturing value added' for assembly elsewhere (perhaps inside ASEAN) or to upgrade in the networks connected with China. Some economists in ASEAN have recently been more upbeat (ERIA 2012), given that it has been observed that China will exhaust its pool of excess cheap labour very soon due to its ageing population and its one-child policy. This trend and the ongoing shift up the value chains will push up Chinese wages rather rapidly – as they are already doing – which is regarded as a golden opportunity for ASEAN to become more attractive for FDI, with the AEC being deepened and widened successfully.

It is demanding to move up. For example, focusing on the (share of) service value-added content in manufacturing in 2009, China, with some 25 per cent, trails all OECD countries and the other BRICs (Brazil, Russia, India, South Africa). Yet Indonesia hardly makes 20 per cent, with a tiny share in business services (De Backer 2013). It is equally important to broaden the sectorial export base, which, again, requires a broader domestic manufacturing base (i.e., not pure export-processing activities, but effective forward and backward linkages spreading to other sectors based on more horizontal capabilities). Thus, judging by one measure of participation in global value chains – foreign inputs in one's own exports, plus domestically produced inputs in the exports of third countries – the Philippines reaches a share of its gross exports of no less than 65 per cent, yet it reflects an extremely narrow specialisation in electronic components and some automotive intermediates. Therefore, their participation in GVCs seems neither to 'move up' nor to widen over more sectors. The country risks becoming stuck in the medium run. Capturing value in such chains is what China has done much better than ASEAN in the last fifteen years (though Japan has done worst by remaining stagnant) as shown in Figure 2.1.

These considerations have kept concerns in ASEAN about the 'middle income country trap' alive, especially for the Philippines, Malaysia and Thailand. The latter two have been growing quite rapidly for many years, and the Philippines has recently joined them after a period of languishing since the fall of Marcos. The concern is about the longer term and 'being squeezed out by the low-wage economies in mature industries, on the one side, and by the more technologically advanced countries specializing on innovation-sensitive sectors on the other ... the dependence on exports as driver of rapid growth, together with the perceived difficulties in carving out a strong global market niche for higher value-added exports, create doubts as to whether these countries could replicate the kind of growth surge that catapulted countries like South Korea to high income status.'[30]

The AEC might be one helpful element in the efforts to escape in the longer term from the middle income country

[30] Quoted from the MICT website, issue paper by Pelkmans-Balaoing (2013). See also Gill and Kharas (2007); ADB Calculations (2010); Eichengreen, Park and Shin (2013).

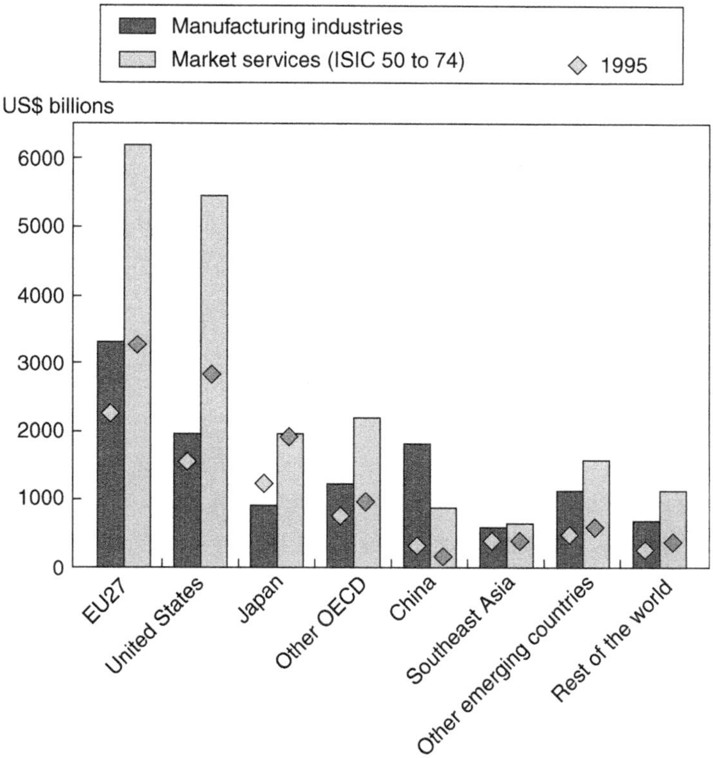

Figure 2.1 Value-added in GVCs of manufactured goods and market services, 1995 and 2009 (US$ billions)
Source: OECD (2013: 20).

trap, but this would work only if accompanied by forceful national education as well as science and technology policies, better public governance and far better technical and physical infrastructures.

The recent work by the OECD (and other international economic organisations) has yielded crucial policy conclusions on GVCs, some of which are worth reiterating for the purpose of making an effective AEC (OECD 2013)

(1) *On trade policy* GVCs imply that trade is mainly about intermediate goods and services; policymakers ought to think of 'activities' not 'industries'; import restrictions are a 'tax' on exports as they make the input in exports more costly; restricting exports can be costly or complicating for GVCs; services are crucial for GVCs – in ASEAN, easily 30 per cent or more of value creation in GVCs comes from services, which means that the competitiveness of the 'activities' hinges on free trade in services and domestic reforms fostering efficiency, competence and trusted quality; for logistics, infrastructure as well as effectiveness and business-friendliness of customs are essential; any FTAs need to encompass a wide range of aspects of GVCs before they are effective handmaidens of competitiveness, that is, services, reduction of NTMs, movement of business people, etc.
(2) *Investment policy*: GVCs may be hindered by the complications of market access for investment from non-ASEAN companies and numerous different bilateral investment treaties (BITs, mainly on investment protection) instead of common investment frameworks; since the WTO has no investment agreement, one might use the OECD Codes (but ASEAN countries are either merely associated with the OECD or have no link whatsoever); incentive wars on acquiring the higher value-added segments of GVCs are self-defeating

(3) *On development policies*: GVCs cannot operate on 'islands' except for simple assembly for exports; this means that a broad-based development policy focusing on opening markets in trade (also services) and investment will have to go together with a favourable business environment (which requires reform efforts in bureaucracy, one-stop shops, etc.), support of technical infrastructure (e.g., testing and certification), higher skilled labour, research centres and management that makes it possible to effectively absorb foreign technology and develop repair facilities, if not variants of intermediate and final products or techniques; since there are many suppliers from several countries, reliable contracting is critical and the ability to enforce contracts is an advantage.

2.5.2 *A pro-competitive quasi-single market for development*

The experience of building AFTA, followed by the conclusion of several FTAs with countries in East and South Asia, has largely removed the fears and hesitations of open development policies. Indeed, AFTA was more or less completely implemented and ASEAN itself has greatly benefited from globalisation in general and East Asian market integration via GVCs and otherwise. Although the focus on GVCs for purposes of development is preponderant in ASEAN, as discussed above, the *national* dimension in such development policies is paramount, even if cooperative approaches are advocated in ASEAN. However, the regional dimension in the form of deeper market integration was lacking before the Bali ASEAN summit. There is likely to be additional merit in exploiting the regional dimension, as the Japanese car producers have done with four ASEAN countries making intermediates which are traded inside ASEAN. Moreover, with higher levels of development, there is also more reason to pursue openness for the purpose of direct trade and FDI in those goods and services sectors where GVCs do not, or hardly, play a role. With all the attention on GVCs in East Asia, it is too often forgotten that GVCs do *not* play much of a role in many goods sectors nor in some service sectors. The quasi-single market also matters in a broader economic perspective. Thus, the sizeable ASEAN region as a whole may well be more attractive for trade negotiations than many national negotiations, which may splinter marketing and logistics strategies of third-country companies.

But also inside ASEAN, there are reasons to intensify market integration with a view to benefiting from the pro-competitive effects of market integration and lowering trade costs in the region. ASEAN has much higher average per capita incomes than two decades ago and a much broader manufacturing and services base. Unlike when AFTA was initiated, twenty-two years ago, ASEAN countries can exchange more products on the basis of refined intra-industry specialisation. Promoting a higher share of intra-ASEAN trade in ASEAN's world trade is accentuating and accelerating a natural development, given the rising incomes in Southeast Asia. With most of ASEAN becoming middle income countries and aiming to reach a status of developed economies in the longer run, intra-ASEAN export patterns will change towards more differentiated manufactured goods emerging from more and more industrial sectors, as well as – to a lesser but growing extent – service exports. This is exactly what one can observe in recent years: the share of resources and agro-goods is shrinking, and that of intermediates and final goods is rising steadily. Such thoughts may be stating the obvious for readers from developed countries – deepening market integration would be expected to boost intra-regional trade. But in the 1980s or 1990s that was not at all obvious for ASEAN. Apart from multinationals using ASEAN as a low wage/low skills base for the labour-intensive segments of value chains, the local specialisation of ASEAN countries was overlapping and imports of final goods from OECD countries were often more attractive due to quality, scale or established brands. What the AEC might be able to do is precisely to accentuate and refine the intra-ASEAN specialisation induced by greater market pressures once NTBs and other regulatory barriers have been drastically reduced. This would be compatible with the greater discretion in the purchasing power of the rising middle classes in ASEAN. For this to work over the medium term, the crucial instrument is to decisively lower 'trade costs' and thereby facilitate market access and effective competition.

The inhibitions to extending such openness to services and investment linger in some countries, but are much less of an obstacle than many years ago. This might have to do with the GVCs conundrum, but equally with the experience in negotiating modern FTAs. Also global and ASEAN business present in ASEAN countries may have exercised pressures in this direction. Recent economic research has demonstrated the potential benefits of such a quasi-single market. For the AEC pursuing a quasi-single market, Rashid *et al.* (2009) have used a computable general equilibrium (CGE) model. Besides making the qualitative case, they find a rise in economic welfare of 5.3 per cent (or US$69 billion), which is more than six times the economic effect of AFTA. Interestingly, all ASEAN countries would benefit though not equally. Extending the AEC to East Asia would add another two-thirds of those initial benefits, with yet another one-third with extensions to the United States and the EU. With all the caveats of CGE modelling, certainly for the complex AEC, these expected gains are by no means trivial, but interesting, if not compelling, for policymakers, citizens and business. It establishes a good case for a quasi-single market, irrespective of the GVCs arguments. Petri, Plummer and Zhai (2012) argue, in an update, that these gains tend to increase over time, similar to our argument above, based on rising incomes leading eventually to intra-industry specialisation. This might relate both to intermediates and final goods, and to a lesser degree to specific services. Another CGE model has been applied by ERIA (2012) with their most ambitious option (only) including zero intra-tariffs, a 20 per cent reduction of the tariff equivalence of services and a 20 per cent reduction of the costs of importing–exporting due to trade facilitation: effects are beneficial and hover between 1 and 3 per cent of GDP. It is an empirical question whether or not ASEAN is capable of delivering a quasi-single market going further than this stylised option; if so, the higher estimates by Petri *et al.* (2012) would become more realistic.

Chapter 3

Conceptual foundation of the ASEAN Economic Community

This section forms an attempt to identify and understand what the AEC actually is. Once again, conceptually. Section 3.1 recalls the Bali Concord II declaration, and section 3.2 the substantive ingredients of the HLTF's recommendations. Section 3.3 attempts to grasp the contents and economic meaning of the Bali 'vision' on the basis of a series of conceptual queries. Section 3.4 summarises the Roadmap for the AEC as published in 2010 in a stylised fashion, with annotations and queries where appropriate as well as a cursory assessment of progress to date, fitting the conceptual analysis.

3.1 The AEC 'vision' declared in Bali

ASEAN is well known for its capacity to deliver elegantly drafted declarations. The Bali Declaration is no exception. If one is willing, one can read a lot in the declaration. In any event, a closer reading demonstrates that Bali amounted to a breakthrough, the more so as it was accompanied by the HLTF recommendations, as an early attempt to flesh out the 'vision' in more operational terms. Figure 3.1 stylises the declaration itself.

Figure 3.1 starts with the cardinal announcement that ASEAN wants deeper, but not 'open-ended', economic

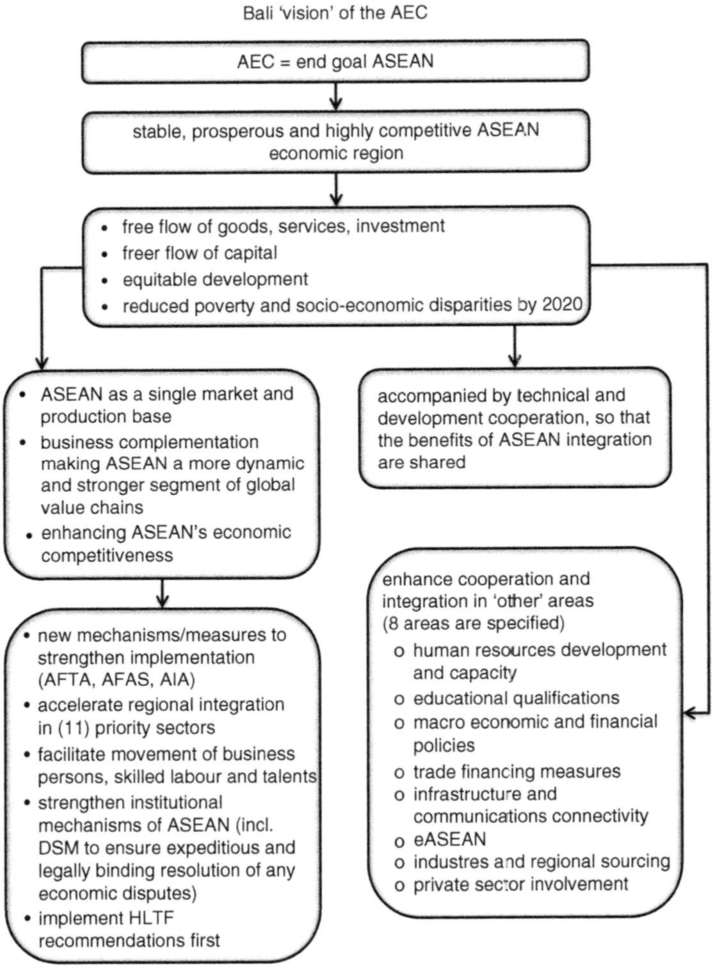

Figure 3.1 Bali 'vision' of the AEC

integration (as the EU, for example). As we shall elaborate in Chapters 4 and 5, this makes the substance of the AEC comparable to that of NAFTA. The overall rationale for the AEC is said to be a 'stable, prosperous and highly competitive ASEAN economic region', an ambitious aim. The third box quotes four aspects (literally), but the first two are 'means' (free flows, or freer flow) and the other two are aspirations. The two 'means' specified might be instrumental for the two aspirations, but this is not *a priori* the case. It might require both national- and ASEAN-level means to ensure this (especially with respect to socio-economic disparities). The declaration mentions 'technical and development cooperation'. So far, intra-ASEAN cooperation in this field has been weak at best, complemented by foreign projects. However, in the cooperation box (right-hand side), one of the nine areas for cooperation is 'human resources development and capacity building'. There is no reference to its funding.

A further specification is found in the upper-left box, namely, a '*single market*' (an extremely ambitious concept) and '*production base*'; business complementation better connecting ASEAN to global value chains (or, perhaps, the other way around) and enhancing ASEAN's economic competitiveness. All these elements hang closely together and overlap in various ways. The spirit of these words seems to reflect a new determination on ASEAN's part to become more attractive as a region for producing intermediate goods and services as a value-added in global value chains. The old, 'organised' forms of government-led complementation would seem to have become discredited (such as the ASEAN Industrial Cooperation scheme (AICO)) and market forces in a single market would lubricate this far more efficiently. The ASEAN single market would both facilitate greatly intra-ASEAN complementation of components and cost-effective 'fragmentation' of the tasks in such chains, whilst also promoting competition and competitiveness in the region more generally. It should also stimulate more liberal arrangements for service provision and, in the medium term, higher quality services (including sophisticated logistics) indispensable for attracting the higher value-added segments of global value chains to ASEAN.

The bottom left-hand box in Figure 3.1 lists five concrete steps that strongly suggest that the political leaders wanted to ensure an immediate and specified follow-up (unlike when AFTA was born in January 1992). The HLTF recommendations will be discussed below, but in any event are quite specific. So is the assignment to ministers to accelerate regional integration in eleven priority sectors. Two items refer both to sensitive aspects of an institutional nature, strengthening implementation and dispute settlement (and other 'institutional mechanisms' without detail). Taking the text at face value, the Bali 'vision' would appear to remedy both weaknesses and thereby raise the credibility and attractiveness of ASEAN internally and for global investors. Finally, mode 4 of GATS is explicitly addressed for the movement of business persons, skilled labour and 'talents'. For an ASEAN-wide business perspective, as well as for the quality aspects of intermediate goods and services production in world-class value chains, a liberal view of mode 4 inside ASEAN is crucial.

3.2 Recommendations from the HLTF

The HLTF recommendations are mostly concrete and of a practical nature. It should be realised that they have gradually been overtaken or adapted by energetic AEC activities in numerous committees, leading to the overall Blueprint and the Roadmap. Nevertheless, it is probably helpful to appreciate better the Bali 'vision' and its practical implementation. The focus is almost entirely on the single market and production base, both via intensifying the (then) current economic initiatives and via new initiatives and measures. There is no attention at all on what would later be called 'integration with the global economy',[1] a cryptic line on IPRs (which in today's Roadmap is regarded as one element of the 'competitive economic region') and two minor items under 'development and technical cooperation'.[2] Although there are timelines as required by the Declaration, there is no blueprint or roadmap yet, not even the intention to draft them.[3] Intensifying existing initiatives amounts to a list of twenty-six proposals, many of which are not new or are already present in 'softer' form. No less than four WTO Agreements should be 'adopted' (nine years after the Uruguay Round ended, those on TBT and SPS, plus those on import licensing and customs valuation), which would merely bring AFTA up to the WTO standard, compulsory for ASEAN countries anyway.[4] Improving origin rules

[1] In the Bali Declaration, items 7, 8 and 9 refer to the external economic dimension.

[2] One is the mobilisation of resources for IAI projects from *within* ASEAN. Surely, this move away from dependence on outside funding would seem to indicate ASEAN's determination to address the development divide, if target amounts for a number of years had been added and/or a common budget increase.

[3] However, roadmaps for each one of the eleven sectors are recommended.

[4] All ten ASEAN countries are now WTO members (Lao since February 2013), but that was not yet the case when the HTLM recommendations

may reduce transaction costs. A shifted target for the removal of NTMs raises doubts because delayed targets look more like ASEAN evergreens – timelines have not helped here, so far. Important proposals on customs, critical for companies' transaction costs and speed of handling, particularly in global or even intra-ASEAN value chains, such as Green Lane systems, a client charter (hopefully changing the mindset of customs officers) and the 'Single Window approach' based on electronic processing. A firm intention on what are called 'standards'[5] is expressed when advocating the completion of MRAs in five sectors (electrical/electronic equipment, cosmetics, pharmaceuticals, telecoms equipment, prepared foodstuffs) and more in future (for sectors with significant trade values), and even new ASEAN technical regulations (a form of 'positive integration'). It should be noticed that the latter recommendation reads 'where possible, for national applications', which leaves one in the dark about the degree of binding.

For trade in services, targets and schedules are advocated in sectors and acceleration is to be based on the ASEAN-X formula. The HLTF also wanted 'MRAs for professional qualifications in major professional services to be completed

were drafted. Nevertheless, some long-standing WTO members of ASEAN have not yet implemented these WTO Agreements.

5 Standards are voluntary market-driven technical specifications – companies are free to adopt them or not, but they often do when standards codify accepted practices or state-of-the-art or accomplish compatibility or interoperability. Technical regulations are laws. Such laws may actually refer to standards for the purpose of clarifying how a desired level of, say, safety or health or environmental performance can be practically achieved.

by 2008', although this area is notoriously difficult. On investment, the five recommendations are modest. The only liberalisation is a shift of sectors in the sensitive list (in 2003) to the temporary exclusion list (TEL), beginning 2004 (i.e., no target date of completion) and based on ASEAN-X. Three items are typical industrial policy interventions,[6] the effectiveness of which is anyone's guess, and one is a very general call for ASEAN investment promotion. Other measures on IPRs (cooperation on copyright) and capital mobility ('expedite' existing Roadmap on Finance in this respect) are very light indeed.

When it comes to new initiatives, the two prominent pillars are the acceleration of integration in the eleven priority sectors and institutional strengthening. The measures for priority sectors are meant to exemplify the process and build up confidence for governments. For goods, the HLTF proposes zero intra-tariffs, immediate removal of 'barriers to trade'(?), faster customs clearance (faster than implied by the customs proposals above?) and acceleration of MRAs' development and harmonisation (regulations and standards). To turn such vague statements into effective economic integration will require a firm strategy and specific commitments by all. For services, proposals are even more vague: accelerated liberalisation in these sectors (the four service sectors are e-ASEAN, healthcare, air travel and tourism) merely indicates

[6] Encourage companies to relocate to (within) ASEAN (sometimes, with incentives), a monitoring mechanism of national investment strategies and establishing a network of ASEAN free trade zones to enhance complementation.

a difference with the prior call for targets and schedules, but without any detail as to accelerated development of MRAs and a call to promote joint ventures, even in third markets. On the mobility of business persons (and tourists), the determination appears to be much greater. A call is made to develop an ASEAN agreement to facilitate movement of business persons and skilled labour (which seems highly useful, as noted), visa exemption for intra-ASEAN travel by ASEAN nationals (by 2005) and the harmonisation of visa policies for non-ASEAN travellers by 2004.

Institutional strengthening is not an empty shell, as sceptics might have expected, but it also confirms some fundamental properties of ASEAN cooperation. The latter is exemplified by the consensus rule, which is explicitly confirmed. What is new is the introduction of an escape route, but the relevant question is whether it will actually be used: 'where there is no consensus, ASEAN to consider other options with the objective of expediting the decision-making process'. There is a miniscule strengthening of the ASEAN Secretariat (a legal unit for legal advice on disputes has been added)[7] and an enhancement of its capability to conduct research and analytical studies (a function now executed by ERIA, with considerable non-ASEAN funding).[8]

The core of the proposals consists of 'an effective system to ensure proper implementation of all economic agreements and expeditious resolution of any disputes' by

[7] See Piris and Woon (2013), for an assessment of the position and role of the legal unit of the ASEAN Secretariat.

[8] See at: www.eria.org.

2004. Knowing how much of a problem this constitutes in ASEAN, both the firm language and the timing (2004) are amazing, to put it mildly. Three recommendations are made: establish ACT (an ASEAN variety of the EU SOLVIT system of informal bilateral problem-solving, with easy access for all); establish an ASEAN Compliance Body (ACB) modelled after the WTO Textile Monitoring Body (based on peer pressure); and an Enhanced ASEAN Dispute Settlement 'making it more practical'. The ACT is certainly a good idea, without affecting the typical ASEAN sensitivities on non-interference in domestic affairs or 'sovereignty'. In the EU, SOLVIT is a success and several reasons for this success could be applied in ASEAN, too.[9] This might apply to ACB as well, but the author has not found a report on its working and performance. The enhanced dispute settlement mechanism (DSM) is seen as a third 'adjudication phase', after the 'advisory' stage (advice from the Secretariat's legal unit and going through

[9] In Pelkmans and Correia de Brito (2012: 20–46), an elaborate analysis of SOLVIT and its results is provided. In 2011, SOLVIT handled some 1,300 cases that fell within its competence, with a resolution rate of nearly 90 per cent and an average duration of seventy days for resolution. Note that SOLVIT is free of charge, easy to access for anybody (business and citizens), and requires adequate resources and skills for the national SOLVIT centres. Cooperation between national administrations has to be quick, and cooperation between SOLVIT and a national administration has to be smooth (and electronic, preferably), with a duty to respond as helpfully as possible in a short time span. Note that the competence of SOLVIT has carefully designed limitations. It is only a partial substitute for dispute settlement. Pelkmans and Correia de Brito denote it as a 'pre-infringement' initiative, that is, preventing infringement procedures by a faster and cost-effective cooperative solution.

ACT) and the 'consultative' stage (ACB). It is noted that this sequence is not compulsory in case of disputes.

ASEAN has wisely opted for new instruments which reflect its preference for non-confrontational problem-solving. It is sensible to rely on two systems of an informal nature, with proven utility, before resorting to DSM. It should be added that, unlike much of the literature on DSM suggests, the emphasis on informal and consultative approaches is not a dead-end street, quite the contrary, as recent experience in the EU demonstrates without any doubt (Correia de Brito and Pelkmans 2012). It is effective once certain conditions are fulfilled. It is also cheap and usually much faster than any form of judicial review. Moreover, Correia de Brito and Pelkmans show in detail and empirically that a further improvement of proper implementation records can best be achieved by careful and extensive 'pre-emptive' approaches. True, this requires intense collaboration, including notification and scrutiny, between the EU member states and the European Commission. To some extent, ASEAN can mimic this as well in future. With one major proviso, of course: these various methods also work well in the EU because there is a credible threat of referral to the CJEU. These considerations are important because the enhanced DSM of the Bali Concord suffers from fatal flaws, and hence little can be expected from it. The HLTF proposes a new DSM modelled on the WTO DSM, including panels made up of independents, an appellate body (idem), a similar selection procedure, strict timelines and the option of sanctions. The problem is that the fatal flaws are omitted in the Bali documents: the reports have to be 'adopted' by ASEAN political organs (ASEAN Economic

Ministers (AEM) and Senior Economic Officials Meeting (SEOM)) in which both parties are represented. Adjudication with political approval is an oxymoron and will simply be avoided. And this is precisely what has happened since.[10]

The HLTF does not offer any interpretation of the conceptual elements of the Bali Declaration, such as 'free flow' or 'freer flow', single (ASEAN) market, production base, equitable development or ASEAN's 'economic competitiveness'.

3.3 Economic concepts of the Bali AEC 'vision'

The link between the great ambition of the Bali Declaration and the specificities of the HLTF proposals seems rather weak, other than expressing a manifest intention to 'act immediately'. This leaves us without any idea of what the defining concepts of the AEC might be. In this subsection, we shall discuss the five economic concepts in the Bali Declaration so as to grasp the economic meaning of the AEC 'vision'. When studying the Roadmap in Chapter 4, it might help readers to assess the nature and extent of the intended economic integration, as expressed in the Roadmap, its numerous detailed technical proposals notwithstanding.

[10] These questions are discussed at much greater length, in more detail and with telling examples by Inama and Sim (2013a). Fundamental issues linked to the ASEAN way of legalisation are also discussed in Davidson (2004) and Ewing-Chow (2008). Pelkmans (1999) reasons that deeper economic integration in ASEAN logically requires a new strategic choice: legalisation for economic integration and the 'ASEAN way' for security and diplomacy.

First, notice the profound ambivalence in the very notion of the 'ASEAN Economic Community' as such. Although ASEAN does *not* aspire to achieve economic integration like the EU, the ASEAN political leaders nevertheless chose to employ highly suggestive language, reminding everyone of the 1957 EEC Treaty. Of course, especially in the ASEAN context, there is a risk of reading too much into this terminology, not least by an author from Europe.[11] Thus, the AEC is like the EEC, 'free flow' would seem to mimic 'free movement' and the single market is presumably even more ambitious than the old 'common market' (the former informally expresses the aspirations of the EU after the first rewrite of the treaty in 1985 and is nowadays employed in Brussels in the Single Market Act[12] as policy language). Even 'equitable development' might have been inspired by similar and permanent EU concerns, expressed as 'harmonious development' (EEC), 'balanced expansion' (EEC) or, more recently, as 'economic and social cohesion' (which refers to what Bali calls 'reduced . . . socio-economic disparities'). Only the 'production base' is unique to ASEAN, given the major role for economic development of the incorporation of ASEAN-based subsidiaries and local suppliers in global value chains.

11 In the discussion of the first draft of this contribution, several ASEAN colleagues expressed surprise about this exegesis of the Bali terminology. According to them, the drafters of the Bali concept of the AEC were interested in an elegant, inspiring idea, not in mimicking the fundamentals of the EEC.

12 See COM(2011) 206, 13 April 2011; for the economic design of the EU internal or Single Market and its stylised progress in accomplishing it over time, see Pelkmans (2011, 2012a).

Whether the tactics of employing EU-like wording has been a wise one, it is difficult to say. There is, of course, a danger of not being taken seriously or of being accused of too much rhetoric, mindful of the huge discrepancy between what ASEAN is known not to want and what leaders appear to be declaring. On the other hand, the similarity to the EEC or EU labels is barely realised or recognised inside ASEAN. Lacking a tradition of rigorous ASEAN lawmaking and case law, the Bali terminology is hardly, or not, perceived as an issue. In the following, I shall nonetheless employ the EU concepts as a benchmark for comparison and clarification, given the assignment of analysing AEC's economic integration from a conceptual point of view.

3.3.1 *What is free flow?*

If 'free movement' is the inspiration for 'free flow', ASEAN would harbour an ambition requiring a revolution in its institutions and rule-making, ending up in a framework much like the EU. Free movement is a radical notion, no other regional group has embraced it. Free movement of goods, services, capital and workers is a *right* for individual economic agents or EU citizens to have unhindered market access to any EU country. EU member states have no legal power to prevent this, except if, and only if, there are derogations in the Treaty (or CJEU case law) that they can invoke (and even then, it ought to be proportional to the – legitimate – objective). It is essentially a federal notion and is strongly pro-competitive.

Free flow is hard to define authoritatively. It would seem to be more than 'free trade' (free from tariffs and quotas) by expecting other barriers to be eliminated as well. But it is precisely those 'other barriers' that have to be identified far more accurately. More important still, it is simplistic, if not misleading, to pronounce that such barriers ought to be eliminated. Many such barriers have regulatory aspects of one kind or another, and the question to ask first is whether a market failure or (exceptionally) another sound justification lies behind each one of them. In ASEAN parlance, apart from various customs issues (ranging from a need for modernisation, to inefficiencies, even to corruption), 'other barriers' have been indicated as NTMs and NTBs. Both are unfortunate terms dating from the early days of trade liberalisation beyond tariffs. These terms have led, and still lead, to semantic debates and a search for criteria about what exactly NTMs are, and – when they are 'trade barriers' – the same for NTBs, although the overlap is large and somewhat arbitrary. It must be said that free flows cannot but imply a fairly ambitious approach to NTBs/NTMs. Such an ambition would be a sea change in ASEAN because this important area of market access barriers (which can be very costly) had never been taken serious before AFTA, not even during the pre-Bali AFTA days. In section 4.1.2 we shall offer some detail on an authoritative classification of NTMs developed by international organisations together (in Box 4.1), solving the ASEAN definition problem, and attempt to come to grips with what ASEAN has done, so far, in addressing TBTs, SPS measures and those NTMs that are not easily justifiable (hence, protectionist).

The guiding rule is that all NTMs *are* trade barriers, that is, they render effective market access more difficult, costly or impossible. The immediate follow-up question is whether they can be justified by 'legitimate' public interest reasons, usually (addressing) 'market failures'. This can be the case with TBTs and SPS measures if certain conditions are fulfilled. Therefore, ASEAN needs a credible system of assessing NTMs, first at the regulatory level (what NTMs are or are not allowed, and, if allowed, under what constraints), and, second, at the judiciary level (assessing whether the avowed public interest reasons for retaining certain NTMs by ASEAN countries are credible, legitimate and compatible with AEC rules of intra-AEC 'free flow'). In the AEC Roadmap, these *principles* driving a long-term programme as well as the *programme* itself are absent. This serious omission has to be corrected. It is hard to believe that this can solely, or even primarily, be attributed to problems of identification or classification of NTMs. Of course, the hard core of NTMs in ASEAN has long been known, if only because UNCTAD has been active on these questions for decades.

We suggest another hypothesis. Broadly, the long drawn-out debate (and lack of action) on ASEAN's NTMs is not so difficult because the term is ill-defined or the criteria are so unclear – although this did make it more problematic – but because long lists of existing NTMs demonstrate the actual protectionism of several, if not most, ASEAN countries. This is particularly true for those NTMs that are not TBTs or SPS measures. Many of these NTMs should have been removed or constrained as part of AFTA once AFTA began to move 'beyond' tariffs. More importantly, one cannot desire an AEC à la Bali and keep a battery of protectionist tools in place. According to a careful survey by Loreli de Dios

(2004), NTMs on the ASEAN list at the time of the Bali Summit included para-tariff measures, price control measures, finance measures (about the modes and timing of payments for imports), quantity control measures (beside quotas, non-automatic licensing, import bans, etc.), monopolistic measures, as well as 'technical measures'. The recent term in ASEAN seems to be the 'core NTMs' (see section 4.1.2 and the data presented there). A possible misfit is the last category. Technical regulations, standards and conformity assessment are not, or at least need not be, 'protectionist', and even if they have been ill-designed, better rules and standards should normally take their place due to market failures. In other words, in most cases they cannot be removed, but the costs of such NTMs for intra-ASEAN trade can be minimised. It is likely to be a misfit, too, because – unlike all others mentioned here – technical regulations have an economic/regulatory logic and dynamism of their own and are often justified by health, safety or the environment (all recognised market failures). True, TBTs may arise because the scope is too widely drawn, or the measures are discriminatory (via opting for specific standards, for example) or otherwise disproportional, and this is precisely a compelling rationale for independent judicial review. TBTs may also arise simply because the technical design of national measures (for similar objectives) is different.

Altogether, 'free flow' is thus unlikely to be an overwhelming 'mother principle' (as free movement is) because how 'free' the flows will be depends on the degree of ambition in addressing NTMs. Furthermore, 'free flow' also concerns services and investment (FDI), which are domains of a regulatory nature, not to mention the 'freer flow' of capital, to be understood as financial capital and portfolio investment. By definition, 'freer' is dependent on one's ambition and therefore 'endogenous'. It will thus be indispensable to have recourse to the Roadmap and observe what the ambitions are in actual practice. Going by the experience of the EU, this ambition (e.g., in goods, regulations, services and investment) may not be fully comprehended initially – in particular, at the national level – which will cause reticence on the part of the ASEAN Member States, even when they are willing. Moreover, when it comes to 'technical regulations', one can safely predict a 'learning-by-doing' process in the emerging AEC, which will intensify over the years far beyond 2015. It took the EU decades of learning how (not) to harmonise and how best to organise European standardisation.[13]

3.3.2 *What is the single ASEAN market?*

It is reasonably well understood what a single market is – see also Table 2.1, stage 6 – but one should not search for a perfect, all-encompassing definition. The latter neither exists in the EU, nor even in federations.[14] What is accepted, is that a single market combines 'deep' and far-reaching cross-border

[13] See Pelkmans (1987a, 1987b). We shall return to these questions in Chapter 4.

[14] In Anderson (2012), five 'internal markets' are studied in a comparative fashion, based on similar analytical approaches: the United States, Switzerland, Canada, Australia and the EU. Although, surely, they have common properties of very 'deep' economic integration, all five are quite distinct when it comes to specifics.

liberalisation, based on the fundamental obligation to ensure mutual market access and non-discrimination, in the five market types one may distinguish (goods, services, capital, labour and codified technology), with ambitious forms and a wide scope of 'positive integration' in both market institutions and regulations.

Going by this understanding, the ASEAN single market would fall far short of it. On codified technology (e.g., IPRs mostly), ASEAN is only just beginning to explore it, and Bali produced no commitments beyond soft cooperation in the form of national policy emulation. On labour, the 'vision' is selective, focusing on skilled labour, but apparently without a right (merely, a facilitation) to access the ASEAN labour markets. On capital, the flows will be 'freer', which contradicts a single market. However, 'investment' is distinguished from 'capital', and it is conceivable (though far from clear in the HLTF report) that a fully free intra-AEC investment regime might eventually be established; without it, it would once again contradict the single market. On services, the Bali Declaration uses wording (free flow) that is in accordance with a single market. However, this accordance hinges on a detailed strategy of both cross-border liberalisation for all modes and common (minimum) regulation as well as relevant common market institutions (say, for certain network industries). Going by the HLTF report, this would seem not to be the case at all. The impression one gets is that the AEC (in services) would eventually consist of a kind of GATS-plus approach, with more ambitious national commitments driven by a common ASEAN strategy. We shall show later that, in fact, the AEC services strategy has become more ambitious over time, prompting the query as to how far it will go by the end of 2015 and indeed later (see section 4.1.3). In goods a single market seems to be inconsistent with the underlying FTA (a customs union would minimise distortions and reduce transaction costs at the intra-ASEAN borders), with the persistent hesitations on NTMs removal and reticence as well as enormous practical questions about common regulation and ASEAN-led standard setting, not to mention implementation and compliance issues. Despite the loose ends in this summing up, there can be no doubt that the AEC as declared in Bali will *not* be a genuine single market – the idea is simply far too ambitious.

A similar conclusion would follow if one were to apply the concepts of economists. The problem is that economists tend to derive their concept from simplistic models. Therefore, the realistic application of such concepts must be subject to a sweeping practical interpretation, due to the enormous gaps between the models and actual market functioning. Lloyd (2005) argues, fitting a long tradition of economic analysis, that an area is completely integrated economically if the 'law of one price' holds for all commodity and factor markets. This empirical criterion has often been tested with respect to the EU internal market for goods (e.g., European Commission 1996; Engel and Rogers 2004; Ilzkovitz *et al.* 2007) as a whole by employing 'price convergence' indicators over time. For the EU, they show that overall (goods) price convergence trends confirm, or at least are consistent with, the gradual deepening and widening of the EU internal market (including tough competition policy at EU and national level). Overall price disparities narrow over time. Nevertheless, Lloyd is forced to interpret the practical conditions for this law also to be even approximately valid in ASEAN, quite similar to the institutional economics of integration inspired by the EU.[15] Indeed, his comparative analysis of seven economic integration processes[16] reveals that only the EU has an almost maximum score for his many 'measures' required for goods, services, capital and labour. There are a number of 'measures' with which one can take issue and crucial ones that seem to have been overlooked,[17] but that exactly confirms the limited utility of basing the exercise primarily on the single price criterion. In any event, many goods and even more services are highly differentiated and, hence, price convergence is exceedingly hard to measure properly in the first place. There is a better case for the price convergence criterion (up to a point) in *specific* goods or well-defined services markets inside an internal market. If price disparities between national markets in such specific goods are persistent and large, this is a sign that 'barriers' persist and/or that anti-competitive market segmentation is practised and competition policy ought to be available to improve market

[15] See Pelkmans (1987c, 2008).

[16] EU, NAFTA, CER, Mercosur, ASEAN, Japan–Singapore FTA, New Zealand–Singapore FTA.

[17] Examples of items that deserve more careful elaboration (and/or are partially incorrect) include the 'harmonisation' measures in goods markets, market access in services and harmonisation of 'business taxes' (where the text refers to equal effective rates, thereby excluding tax competition – there is also no clear distinction with the more important harmonisation of the corporate tax base, the lack of which is often highly distortive). Examples of neglect include, e.g., the absence of host-country control for cross-border migration of labour, and no mention of common regulation in many services markets (at times, complemented with common agencies), without which no single services market could ever emerge.

functioning. The McKinsey report (2003) showed that price disparities inside ASEAN are rife.[18] The ASEAN single market could help to mitigate these, insofar as its practical elaboration by 2015 or beyond can generate the cross-border intra-ASEAN competitive pressures to make this happen. In some finished goods and the more tradable services, price convergence might happen in the future, but, as the EU examples exemplify, in numerous goods and services markets, not to mention labour, the sufficient requirements to obtain price convergence are very ambitious indeed.

There is a second approach to detect whether an economic area is approaching a 'single market', namely, 'home bias'.[19] Home bias is based on a pure integration benchmark. In a truly integrated market, economic agents from country A (member of the integrated group) would assume a group-wide outlook in all economic decisions, hence, purchase a share of intermediate and final goods domestically reflecting the relative

[18] For the EU, a telling example includes the evolution of the EU car market from being highly segmented (Hocking 1980) to becoming gradually convergent in prices of identical cars, after three decades of harmonisation, adaptation of EU competition policy exemptions and EU standardisation; for a rigorous examination, see Goldberg and Verboven (2005). Also consider the EU telecoms services market for which Pelkmans and Renda (2011) have demonstrated huge price disparities for eleven leading, more or less standardised eComms services, despite extensive common regulation and EU competition policy. In fact, the authors conclude that the common regulation has liberalised *national* markets, with significant economic benefits, but has done little to achieve a single eComms market – this would require a common EU agency (very sensitive) and more intrusive EU rules.

[19] The following paragraph is adapted from Pelkmans (2008).

size of the country in that group's economy, the remainder would be purchased from the other countries of the group. Corrections of this ideal purchasing behaviour can be used in the empirical testing, such as a common language (lowering trade costs) between two or more countries of the group, contiguity between two or more countries of the group (greater familiarity and better information) or business networks or, for example, sectorial differences (e.g., Chen 2004). For the EU, empirical research has shown that 'home bias', even when controlled for all such factors, is quite high, in other words, the single market still seems a little remote when observing company behaviour. Nevertheless, trends are clearly downwards – market integration deepens[20] over time. In her comparison with the US market, Pacchioli (2011) finds that the EU home bias in the EU is about three to four times as large as between US states. Unfortunately, home bias is an appealing idea if the bias is very large as this would clearly contradict with a single market, but it tends to become arbitrary at lower levels of bias. The reason is that it has no theoretical economic underpinning. It seems quite hard to derive practical interpretations (as Lloyd has done for the law of one price) for the institutional and regulatory conditions of a single (ASEAN) market from the notion of 'home bias'.

The conclusion is that ASEAN is likely to develop its own *sui generis* form of a single market, which should neither be interpreted in a rigorous economic fashion nor be expected to be anywhere near to that of the EU.

[20] A decline of home bias over time is found by Head and Mayer (2000); Nitsch (2000); Delgado (2006).

3.3.3 *Production base*

There can be little doubt that ASEAN hopes to reinforce its position as an attractive regional production base, an alternative to and/or a complement of China basically. ASEAN presumably envisages a region in which there are increased backward and forward linkages amongst various production facilities and networks that are dispersed throughout Southeast Asia. As ASEAN countries exhibit different endowments, levels of development and capacity, a dynamic division of labour can be developed amongst them if a smooth and efficient cross-border exchange of inputs to production can be assured. Eliminating intra-ASEAN barriers should play an important role in facilitating this exchange. However, the dynamic division of labour amongst ASEAN countries will result from sustained flows of direct investment, including the relocation of industries from more developed to less developed ASEAN countries, and the continuous expansion and upgrading of regional production networks. A single production base in the region implies that production activities in each one of the ASEAN countries will become (more) regionalised, if not internationalised at the same time. It would also imply that the prior and/or subsequent connections to the ASEAN-based production are as critical as the intra-ASEAN liberalisation and facilitation. That means that the links with East Asia and presumably other critical trade and investment partners such as the EU and the United States have to be deepened simultaneously with the deepening and strengthening of the ASEAN production base. Whereas developing the ASEAN 'single market' might suggest a strong focus on internal 'deepening', given the enormity of the task, the ASEAN 'production base' strongly suggests some combination of intra-ASEAN deepening of market integration (without necessarily going all the tiring and sensitive way towards a genuine single market) and selective business-friendly market integration with leading trading partners in East Asia and beyond.

The clear intention to accord priority to an internationalised value-chains agenda for ASEAN renders it more difficult to be systematic and impose coherence in the AEC programme. One may suggest a minimum agenda for goods and services markets as well as investment, plus a range of desires with respect to intra-ASEAN economic cooperation and infrastructure, but the menu would always remain pragmatic and, indeed, somewhat differentiated between the ASEAN countries, in contrast to the defining idea of a 'single market'. Building a competitive production base is likely to be prioritised slightly differently in the eyes of business than by ASEAN as a group. Thus, international and ASEAN-based business perceives cross-border liberalisation as less urgent (perhaps because it is slow and cumbersome, in packages, etc.) than trade facilitation, mainly because in ASEAN there are huge potential gains to be reaped by ambitious trade facilitation (see section 4.3 for evidence).

The Bali Declaration mentions a single market and production base together. For non-ASEANs this formulation is not immediately obvious. There have been soundings that the single market would be meant primarily for consumers and the production base for the supply side. The political economy of launching the 'twins' in the region is often said to be the following: the strong ASEAN and multinational business pressures to improve ASEAN as a production base had to be 'balanced' by an appealing concept for consumers. However, that would be a curious, if not mistaken, approach. The deeper market integration, the more these two sides will be intertwined to such a degree that such a distinction becomes pointless. But even when market integration fails to become very 'deep', one cannot really separate the two. For one, barriers to a single market will hit the production side, probably more often than consumption because, for example, some NTMs (including, in particular, technical barriers), many service restrictions and investment restrictions are targeted to supply-side activities. Second, in the final analysis, consumption is likely to be affected by supply restrictions, too, unless local inputs in value chains are incorporated in goods or more advanced inputs which are entirely exported. Of course, ASEAN has many 'export processing zones' and if they are kept insulated from the rest of the local or national economy, the developmental effect will also remain quite limited. Indeed, it might perpetuate the location of low value-added production in such zones and thereby risk falling into the 'middle income trap', surely not the vision of the ASEAN leaders.[21] Viewing the single market as more or less

[21] Following from an earlier note on this problem (Chapter 2, fn. 30) the 'middle income trap' refers to the limits of an outward development strategy geared to attracting relatively low-skilled production as segments of global value chains, without more than marginal economic supply connections with the local economy. The initial growth success of such strategies risks turning into a 'trap' yielding only moderate further development (hence, little catch-up with OECD countries) unless one succeeds in adapting market access and localisation policies whilst inducing upward shifts in the segments of the value chains. It might explain why the AEC 'vision' also includes what are basically 'domestic' policies, such as up-skilling the labour force as well as education more generally.

separate, would suggest that the ASEAN-based segments of global value chains have little or no connection with local consumption or local production of consumption goods, and that intermediate inputs cannot be sold locally at all. The developmental impact presumably comes with more and higher quality backward and forward linkages with the economy of location. The higher the level of development, the less likely it is that the separation of 'single market' and 'production base' makes sense. Since ASEAN as a group has experienced healthy growth since the 1997 crisis, by now this separation might be relevant only to some remote areas in ASEAN and to Lao, Myanmar and Cambodia.[22] For non-ASEAN observers, it might therefore be more useful, when attempting to understand this dual-track formulation, to regard the production base as a market-driven instance of modern *development policy*, but jointly in ASEAN, as this common approach is potentially more attractive for multinationals. It would seem that, in emphasising this market-driven dual track, ASEAN has finally broken with its old habit of highly interventionist joint forms of 'complementation'.

[22] Thus, Ishida (2009) discusses in detail the spread of existing and new special economic zones in these three countries and Vietnam, partly linked to the Greater Mekong Subregion Economic Cooperation programme. It is not uninteresting to note that economic growth rates for 2011–13 (2013 ADB forecasts) in ASEAN are highest for Lao (8 per cent), Cambodia (6.5 per cent) and Myanmar (6 per cent), equal to Indonesia, probably due in part to trade-generating FDI inflows to such zones. Landingin and Wadley (2005) analyse the stimulating interaction between the 'growth triangle' in East ASEAN (southern tip of the Philippines with Indonesia and East Malaysia/Brunei) and export processing zones, in particular, by complementarities with the local economies.

3.3.4 *What is equitable development in the AEC?*

Income per capita disparities between countries in ASEAN are unusually sharp. Ignoring Singapore as an outlier, disparities are mitigated but remain relatively large compared with other regional groups. However, it should not be forgotten that ASEANs are exposed to large *domestic* income per capita disparities as well. This might perhaps indicate that the sensitivity to disparities is not as great as it is in relatively more egalitarian countries such as South Korea, Japan or, for that matter, Canada and the EU countries. Whatever the explanation, 'equitable development' in the AEC is to some extent a legacy from the history of ASEAN and AFTA, including the special position of the CMLV countries, and to some extent it might be regarded as a new concern if, and to the extent that, the AEC's core strategy (single market and production base) might generate a widening of the development divide. As noted, recent real economic growth rates in the CMLV countries are quite high and, if sustained, the development gap might well be narrowed in ASEAN. Narjoko, Kartika and Wicaksono (2009) are optimistic in this respect and ascribe the recent catch-up trends in ASEAN to the rapidly increased participation in international production networks. They observe that the comparative advantage of more developed ASEAN countries has shifted towards higher segments of the value chain and relatively low-skilled, labour-intensive production is relocating to the CMLV countries. It is suggested that the AEC could support, if not accentuate, these trends leading to a further narrowing of the development gap inside ASEAN.

It is no secret that the political approach to the development gap affecting CMLV countries has always remained relatively unimpressive. It consists mainly of temporary exemptions or delayed deadlines in tariff liberalisation schedules and the AISP programme of preferences (which has been eroded due to ever lower tariffs). The underlying issues of underdevelopment and capacity problems are unlikely to be addressed in earnest in these short 'grace periods'. ASEAN has traditionally done very little about crippling capacity or infrastructure constraints in the poorest member countries, other than appealing to non-ASEAN donors for technical or development aid. According to Chia (2007), neither the Initiative for ASEAN Integration (IAI) nor the ASEAN Development Fund (ADF, where it was hoped that foreign donors would 'leverage' ASEAN seed money) has proven to be successful.[23] Therefore, how should one read the Bali Declaration when it says that: 'The AEC shall ensure that deepening and broadening integration of ASEAN shall be accompanied by technical and development cooperation in order to address the development divide and accelerate the economic integration of the CMLV . . .'? As noted, the HLTF merely specifies two very minor recommendations, one on resources from *within* ASEAN (but without a strategy, no clear commitments by all and no budget, what does this mean?), and one on an extension of the coverage of AISP products. Is it window dressing for reasons of political symbolism or the beginning of a genuinely new approach? It is

[23] One cannot be surprised about the ADF when ASEAN countries started with (equal!) contributions of no more than US$1 million as seed money.

interesting to remember that at the outset the EEC also declared the goal of 'harmonious development' (i.e., avoiding a development gap), and de facto practised a market-driven approach, which initially worked rather well (e.g., with Italy catching up). EU regional policy (with an EU Regional Fund) only started in 1975, and became significant only in the late 1980s with the much more powerful Structural and Cohesion Funds.[24]

3.3.5 *What is ASEAN's economic competitiveness?*

The Bali Declaration states that: 'ASEAN's strategy shall consist of the integration of ASEAN and enhancing ASEAN's economic competitiveness.' There is little else in the Declaration and the word (ASEAN) competitiveness does not even return in the HLTF report.[25] Although somewhat vague, the sentence probably refers once again to the single market (i.e., ASEAN integration) and ASEAN as a production base (enhancing economic competitiveness). From an economic perspective, this is a slightly misleading formulation. *Both* the single market and production base, if pursued

[24] Whilst it is not suggested that the EU 'cohesion' strategy is the example to follow for ASEAN, it is nevertheless useful for a better appreciation of employing explicit policies to pursue 'equitable development' to know that the annual expenditure of the four funds under the EU approach is around €40 billion. It is largely spent on hard and soft infrastructure as well as the more costly public environmental projects.

[25] Other than a reference to the title of the 2003 McKinsey report (ASEAN Competitiveness report).

ambitiously, are effective instruments to 'enhance' ASEAN economic competitiveness. That is, if 'competitiveness' is understood, as it often implicitly is, as the capacity of an economy to generate steady economic growth via competitive markets, complemented by both domestic and (here) ASEAN-level instruments of regulation, policies and subsidies for non-market activities (such as good and accessible public education at lower and medium levels) consistent with such a long-term strategy.[26] When *domestic* policies and budgets target policies such as education and training as well as infrastructure, which are likely to underpin 'competitiveness', the *ASEAN level* of policymaking can contribute to 'competitiveness' precisely by means of establishing a single market and stimulating the common production base. Together, this should fuel competition and improve company-level productivity, in turn usually generating economic growth in the short term and the restructuring of industries in the longer term. In the longer term, the overall level of productivity is raised by what is called 'market selection', the rising share of the more productive firms and the shrinking or exit of less productive companies within and between sectors. In rapidly growing economies, this restructuring and sectorial change can remain relatively smooth as human and financial resources can find employment elsewhere relatively easily.

[26] For economists, 'competitiveness' is a concept fitting a company, much less a sector and not a country. Nevertheless, competitiveness councils, reports and policies have been found all over the world for decades. Business and political leaders are fond of 'competitiveness'. It is this implicit meaning of (here, ASEAN) competitiveness which is presumably referred to in Bali.

Following Bali, enhancing competitiveness has become a separate chapter in the Roadmap. In terms of calendars and the commitments of ASEAN countries, this might be defendable, but it remains curious to maintain an artificial split between two combined ASEAN instruments fostering competitiveness in the region and 'other' tools to enhance it. It is probably best read as complementary to the two core means of the AEC, that is, the single market and the production base, presumably with an emphasis on the latter.

3.4 How the Roadmap elaborates the AEC concepts

Following Bali, ASEAN has not stood still. A detailed Roadmap was developed (ASEAN 2010).[27] It is more structured than the HLTF report and attempts to flesh out the route to the completion of the AEC in 2015. Also, its coverage is much wider and its degree of detail in all these policy domains makes it a true 'workhorse' for decision makers.

However, there is a 'many trees or the forest' type of problem: rather than inspecting each and every proposed measure (some 300), we shall ask conceptual questions about what 'forest' the Roadmap seems to be aiming for.

A first observation is the stimulus for deepening and widening that the AEC 'vision' has generated in ASEAN. The Roadmap is more ambitious than the various action plans

[27] In fact, the three Blueprints, one for the AEC and the two other communities (political–security, socio-cultural) are together denoted as the Roadmap. In the text, we merely refer to the part of the Roadmap relevant for the AEC.

ASEAN used to adopt without much effect (Hanoi; Vientiane) before Bali. Moreover, even when one retains a degree of scepticism about implementation and enforcement, it is true that the Roadmap comprises a number of what ASEAN calls 'Agreements'. These are forms of positive integration that are binding in the sense that they require incorporation into domestic law of the Member States, a process called 'ratification'. One might regard such Agreements as an intergovernmental counterpart of what the EU calls 'directives',[28] except that EU law is (largely) centrally enforced with precision. Such Agreements, other than in AFTA, were rare before Bali. In addition, the Roadmap contains several 'ASEAN directives'(!), such as on cosmetics regulation and on medical devices, which textually look very similar to technical EU directives. Without having studied these initiatives in detail, it would seem that ASEAN Agreements are primarily about liberalisation (with some minor positive integration), whereas 'ASEAN directives' are clearly instances of technical harmonisation.[29] ASEAN has also opted for MRAs in some goods markets, presumably because they are a

[28] A directive, once adopted by the EU legislature (the Council and the European Parliament together), is binding with respect to purpose and effects. In actual practice, however, EU directives are quite detailed and recently (at least, for the internal market) the trend is to employ EU regulations (which have direct effect on companies and citizens) without passing through the national legislatures.

[29] See Reyes (2013) for a detailed study of the ASEAN cosmetics directive and its implementation in the Philippines. The author finds that the tougher technical requirements and fully-fledged, internationally respectable conformity assessment have raised the costs of introducing cosmetics into the domestic market to such a degree that many small- and medium-sized enterprises (SMEs) tend to be squeezed out of the market. Because

relatively non-intrusive form of overcoming (one class of) technical or regulatory barriers[30] in goods markets (compared with the much more difficult and slow harmonisation of the technical rules themselves). ASEAN has also developed MRAs in professional services, which are not comparable with those in goods as they deal with diploma recognition (e.g., of professionals).

the multinationals are comfortable with these high health and safety standards – indeed, the author suggests that ASEAN harmonisation is forcefully supported by them – it amounts to a classical instance of 'raising rivals' costs'. On the other hand, refusing such regulation is tantamount to allowing unsafe products into the Philippines' market.

[30] As in the WTO, MRAs in goods markets set quality criteria for testing and certification bodies (say, in B), which can then be 'recognised' by MRA partner A for certification of goods to be exported to A. However, this certification in country B for export to A is strictly based on the technical regulations (and possibly, standards) of A, in other words, there is no harmonisation. Thus, testing of good X for market A may well be different to that for market B. MRAs require a lot of trust in sensitive goods (chemicals, food, certain electrical goods, medical devices, etc.) markets and often lead to extra inspections. The idea is to save on the costs of testing and certification in the destination country (if goods are not very small, so that transport costs are high or require continuous testing verification). Many MRAs in the world do not function well due to problems of trust or interpretation issues or lack of delegation from regulators. It is probable that ASEAN has been prompted by the APEC initiatives on MRAs in the late 1990s (in turn, strongly suggested by the US telecoms industry, and later by companies in value chains for electric and electronic goods in East Asia) on telecoms equipment and electric/electronic goods. However, these MRAs have, respectively, two and three stages, and therefore do not lead immediately to lower transaction costs. Lower trading costs are accomplished only in stage 2 (telecoms) or stage 3 (electronic). See also the ASEAN Framework Agreement on Mutual Recognition Agreements, available at: http://www.aseansec.org/6674.htm.

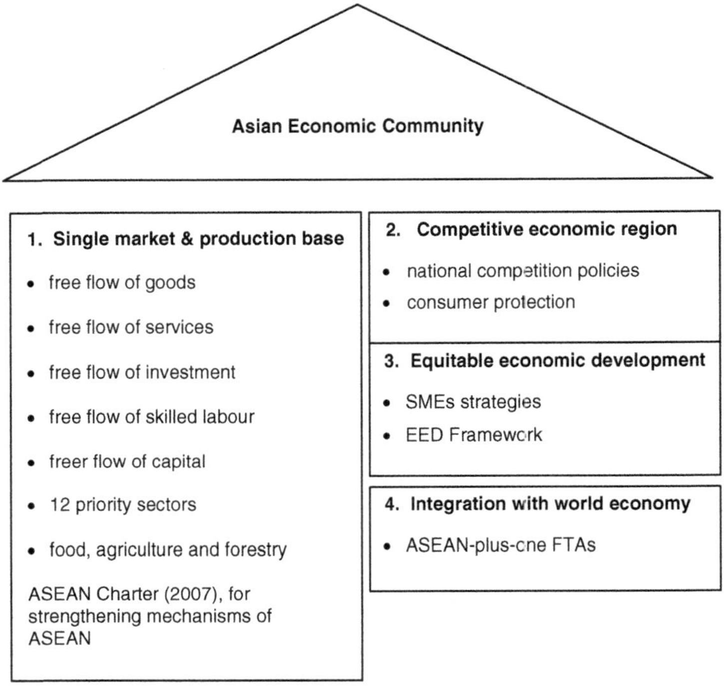

Figure 3.2 ASEAN Economic Community

Second, it would seem that the Bali 'vision' has been extended somewhat in the better structured Roadmap currently followed. Figure 3.2 helps one to see the 'forest'. The AEC has now four parts: single market and production base; competitive economic region; equitable economic development; and integration into the world economy. The fourth part was only implicit (see fn. 1, above) in Bali. The full title in the Roadmap is telling: 'Coherent approach towards external economic relations and enhanced participation in global supply networks.'

The second part (competitive economic region) is, strictly speaking, inconsistent with Bali. As Figure 3.2 shows, the overall *aim* of the AEC is to create a (stable, prosperous and) highly competitive economic region. In the Roadmap, the competitive economic region has turned into an instrument. The same label stands for a short list of diverse actions and is separate from the hard core, the single market and production base. Economically, it is hard to defend such a structuring, though in actual ASEAN practice it might have more to do with jealously kept national regulatory autonomy in these domains as well as the financing of common infrastructure. In the first part, there are now twelve priority sectors, food/agriculture/forestry has been added separately and the institutional strengthening (especially, the enhanced dispute settlement mechanism (EDSM)) is not incorporated in the Roadmap because it has been addressed in the 2007 ASEAN Charter. In terms of economic importance and relevance of the four parts to the AEC concept, as observed, our Figure 3.2 purposefully deviates from the picture of the four 'equal' pillars employed in the AEC Scoreboard (ASEAN 2012: 16). Figure 3.2 conveys much better what matters for the AEC.

Third, since (almost by ASEAN tradition) the Bali Declaration did not specify what 'free flows', 'freer flow' or, indeed, the single market or the production base or, for that matter, competitive economic region in the instrumental sense, can be understood to mean (and the HLTF report did not help in this respect), it is indispensable to scrutinise the Roadmap's details and the many ongoing follow-ups of specialised ministerial meetings. Table 3.1 summarises the Roadmap as published in 2010. However, it is amended or

Table 3.1 *A summary of the 2012 AEC Roadmap*

1.	Single market and production base
1.1	Free flow of goods - tariff reduction/elimination (sensitive, highly sensitive lists, acceleration priority sectors; reduce general exceptions list) implement ATIGA; - elimination of NTBs (2010–12 ASEAN-6); stocktaking and updating NTMs; - rules of origin; (simplify) implement ATIGA; ROO improvements; pilots on 'self-certification'; - trade facilitation; 'harmonise and standardise trade and customs process, procedures'; - customs facilitation, many measures, e.g., ASEAN customs documents, ASEAN customs transit system, ASEAN cargo processing model, pre-arrival clearance, ASEAN harmonised tariff nomenclature, ASEAN Single Window (seven countries); - reduction in technical barriers via harmonisation of national rules, ASEAN (recognised) standards, enhancing technical infrastructure, MRAs on conformity assessment in selected sectors.
1.2	Free flow of services - liberalisation of services flows (mode 1 and 2) and 'substantially no restriction for establishing (intra-ASEAN FDI)'; - eight packages of flows liberalisation in AFAS by 2012 (then eighty service subsectors; all subsectors in 2015); ninth package expected in 2013; - gradual rise (to 70 per cent) of minimally allowed foreign (ASEAN) equity participation, with four priority sectors first, plus logistics, by 2015 for other sectors; - MRAs for seven professional services providers, other MRAs foreseen; - mode 4 for ASEAN Agreement on Movement of Natural Persons (November 2012); - detailed actions in several modes of transport (air and maritime shipping);

Table 3.1 (*cont.*)

	- financial services liberalisation prudent, based on ASEAN-X, and to be continued until 2020, five packages accomplished so far, a sixth package expected by 2014, more on insurance, too; see also 'freer capital' (1.4).
1.3	Free flow of investment
	- combines liberalisation, 'better' regulation of investment and common investment promotion;
	- ASEAN Comprehensive Investment Agreement (ACIA) now ratified; in force since March 2012; schedules to reduce 'reservation lists' in process during 2012; a 'peer review' amongst ASEAN Member States should help this process;
	- ACIA comprises enhanced investment protection, facilitation and cooperation (voluntary harmonisation to support 'complementation'; simpler procedures, single stops) promotion and liberalisation of access;
	- liberalisation of FDI based on 'free and more open' investment regime, non-discrimination (national treatment and MFN) initially still limited, to be widened later over more sectors; free entry in five priority sectors (including industry and agriculture) not yet accomplished.
1.4	Freer flow of capital
	- five rounds of financial services liberalisation completed; sixth one ongoing since 2011, expected in 2014, see 1.2 above (services);
	- capital market development is about deepening equities markets (e.g., ASEAN exchanges) and ASEAN bond markets; Credit Guarantee and Investment Facility initiated; ASEAN Infrastructure Fund (US$500 million) linked to bond markets (2011);
	- the liberalisation of capital movements guided by: (i) orderly capital account liberalisation, (ii) adequate safeguards against potential macro-economic instability and systemic risk, (iii) benefits to be shared by all ASEAN countries;
	- harmonisation for integrated capital market back-loaded for 2014–15;

Table 3.1 (*cont.*)

	– liberalisation of non-ASEAN FDI and (even more) portfolio investments highly conditional ('where applicable, appropriate, possible', etc.); reticence in wording of Strategic Schedule; soft call to eliminate 'dual exchange rates'; the end stage of 'freer flow' undefined.
1.5	Free flow of skilled labour
	– see services Agreement on Movement of Natural Persons.
1.6	Twelve priority sectors
	– acceleration of tariff cuts, plus sector strategies (industrial policy, such as for automotive products, ASEAN tourism strategic plan).
1.7	Food, agriculture and forestry
	– food security framework (including SPS measures, food standards in processing, HACCP, inspections, and food regulatory harmonisation);
	– forest certification by 2015 to combat illegal logging/trade and forest fires.
2.	Competitive economic region
2.1	Competition policy
	– Handbook, Guidelines and expert group on (national) competition policy;
	– 'endeavour' to introduce competition policy in all ASEAN countries by 2015.
2.2	Consumer protection
	– cooperative approach and networking of consumer protection agencies;
	– notification of 'banned' products ('rapid alert');
	– ASEAN website on consumer redress for cross-border purchases.
2.3	Intellectual property rights (IPRs)
	– ASEAN IPR Action Plan, more assertive plan adopted in 2012 (until 2015).
2.4	ASEAN infrastructure

Table 3.1 (*cont.*)

	- transport broad strategies in Brunei Action Plan and ASEAN Connectivity; specific liberalisation of modes (ASEAN Open Skies, ASEAN Shipping market), step by step – see 1.2 above; ASEAN Highway Network;
	- ASEAN ICT Master Plan, including Broadband Corridor;
	- ASEAN Plan of Action on Energy Cooperation (seven programmes, including ASEAN Power Grid, ASEAN Gas Pipeline).
2.5	Taxation
	- complete network of bilaterals inside ASEAN preventing double taxation by 2010 (not completed by December 2011).
3.	Equitable economic development
3.1	- SME strategies and building up of quality culture;
3.2	- Initiative for ASEAN Integration (IAI), focusing on CMLV and two 'growth triangles' and (in 2010) ASEAN Framework on Equitable Economic Development.
4.	Integration into world economy
4.1	Deepening trade and investment relations with leading trading partners, via ASEAN-Plus-One FTAs (five concluded, two under negotiation by December 2011); November 2012 RCEP was initiated, the East Asian network of FTAs driven by 'ASEAN centrality' – the idea is to gradually achieve greater convergence of rules and compatibility between the FTAs.

updated where official documents show progress or elaboration more recently (until spring 2013). Indeed, the substance of the Roadmap still deepens and may occasionally widen as well. This can be appreciated when studying the newest Scorecard report (ASEAN 2012) which lists a number of precisions or new Agreements or other specifications not present in the earlier Roadmap.[31] Where ministerial meetings are known to have taken decisions going beyond the text of the 2010 Roadmap, we have incorporated these developments where relevant until mid 2013. In the main text following this Table, and going through most of these policy areas, more recent developments have been included in the text until mid-2015, in the specialised subsections which follow.

This ASEAN approach to the AEC defies to some extent the economic logic of policy-making. This logic would have political leaders and parliaments define the overall (economic) aims of the AEC, identify the 'instrumental objectives' to bring this about in the longer run, and subsequently the technical, economic and legal instruments which would – together – amount to the implementation of the AEC so as to make it credible and function effectively in order to achieve the overall economic aim(s).[32] Relying on this logic for the AEC, one has to engage in some interpretation as follows. The overall economic aim of the AEC is formulated in Bali: ASEAN as a stable, prosperous and highly competitive economic region. The five 'instrumental objectives' employed to achieve this aim over time have been discussed in section 3.3: free flow(s); single ASEAN market; ASEAN as a production base; equitable development in the

[31] However, the Roadmap itself is not updated, as far as we know. It must be said that the ASEAN website, though much improved compared with, say, a decade ago, does not always provide the information or does so much later than decisions are announced as having been taken.

[32] This traditional approach has been inspired by economists such as Nobel Laureate Jan Tinbergen (1956).

region; and (a more instrumental approach to) ASEAN's economic competitiveness. These five are interrelated as has been discussed above and, hence, are not fully independent,[33] but they may still be helpful for an understanding of the build-up phase of the AEC. However, they clearly require careful inspection at the detailed instrumental level on the basis of the Roadmap. This inspection of the 'implementation level' is the subject of Chapter 4.

[33] So, strictly speaking, the Tinbergen logic (used for modelling, for instance) would require independent instruments.

Chapter 4

Implementation of the AEC: progress in adopting instruments from the Roadmap

Adopting and elaborating instruments from the Roadmap is a major technical implementation exercise, indispensable for the emergence of a workable AEC. The following will offer a detailed scrutiny of the implementation of three of the five 'instrumental objectives': free flows, the single ASEAN market and ASEAN as a production base. Progress is incorporated up to the spring of 2013.

4.1 Implementing the free flows

The Roadmap clarifies the ambitions of the 'free flows' to be accomplished for goods, services, investment and skilled labour.

4.1.1 Implementing the free flow of goods and ATIGA

With respect to goods, the Roadmap goes far beyond what one might expect from AFTA. A fifteen-item customs modernisation and cooperation programme (including cargo processing and a transit system) and a range of trade facilitation measures demonstrate this ambition. The complex patchwork of AFTA/CEPT measures has been integrated into ATIGA. ATIGA is surely an improvement in substance and it is convenient and more transparent than the AFTA patchwork for business and others. Tariffs inside ASEAN are hardly the problem anymore, and MFN tariffs have come down as well during the construction of AFTA. Moreover, applied tariffs are usually lower still. We are only unclear about export taxes (assuming that they are not seen as NTMs), of importance given the recent extensions of such taxes on, for example, minerals by Malaysia and Indonesia.

The problem is another one. Article 1 of ATIGA sets the bar very high in stating that the 'objective of this Agreement is to achieve free flow of goods in ASEAN ... by 2015.' On this account, one can criticise ATIGA because neither the full obligations are guaranteed for that purpose nor the institutional conditions would seem to be fulfilled. Some of the lingering problems of ATIGA are explained in Box 4.1, based on an elaborate and careful legal and institutional analysis by Inama and Sim (2013a) from which we quote or paraphrase freely. We have chosen to emphasise these shortcomings in a separate box for the obvious reason that ATIGA's ambition is critical to the performance of ASEAN segments of global value chains, quite apart from 'free flow' being the core of a single market. In the final analysis, whatever the services and skill input in value-added in global value chains, what is decisive for business is to easily, if not freely, move goods in and out of countries in the region.

4.1.2 *The free flow of goods and addressing NTMs*

The Roadmap is confusing and highly deficient with respect to actions about removal or disciplining NTMs. In the main text, item 14 speaks of 'elimination of Non-Tariff Barriers', indeed, by

Box 4.1 ATIGA shortcomings for accomplishing the 'free flow of goods'

Some goods remain on the exclusion list such as rice and sugar. Based on the GATT Enabling Clause (as AFTA was), some of the goods trade liberalisation inside ASEAN would not be GATT-compliant had ATIGA been notified under Article 24 (as is the routine for regional agreements in the WTO). ATIGA does not contain any provision for actually implementing the 'free flow' in the areas of TBT and SPS. ATIGA has no new dispute settlement of its own (unlike for investments in ASEAN where arbitrage will apply), hence, only the EDSM remains available with its serious weaknesses. ATIGA has not removed the old reciprocity clauses from the pre-AFTA days, which might be a problem if ever conflicts should arise in the AEC for goods (in fact, it has also caused a 'me too' reaction with some other ASEAN countries when Malaysia put automotive products on the Temporary Exclusion List, with more restrictions as a result; placement on the List is actually a unilateral decision which is, of course, contrary to the road towards 'free flow'). For NTBs, there is a risk of 'reverse discrimination', giving better treatment to some non-ASEAN countries in FTAs with them than inside ASEAN (thereby denying the MFN obligation). The red tape around certificates of origin, including conscious intolerance by customs of trivial or petty issues, has been partly, but not fully, addressed in appendix 8 of ATIGA. Moreover, some technical issues around origin have not

Box 4.1 (cont.)

been resolved. ASEAN is de facto split on self-certification for customs purposes, a major cost saver for regular traders and multinationals (hence, for value chains). An attempt is being made to overcome the split on self-certification by two pilots begun in 2014, each with a different group of ASEAN member states. The aim is to arrive at an ASEAN-wide self-certification system by 2015. Customs valuation (regulated under a WTO Agreement) still creates problems inside ASEAN, exemplified by the Philippines–Thailand cigarettes WTO dispute settlements case. The ASEAN Single Window, crucial for ATIGA, of course, is legally still under negotiation and at least eleven complex questions wait to be resolved. However, as Figure 4.2 shows, actual progress has been made in the ASEAN-5. The more general problems of proper implementation and enforcement are highly relevant for ATIGA given the technical nature and specifics of ATIGA, yet it remains to be seen how the expected (and actual) 'implementation gap' and 'enforcement deficit' can be effectively overcome for business to be more confident. After all, this gap and that deficit are a function of the general reluctance of ASEAN nations to accept either hard litigation rules and practices (also against national authorities), as in, for example, NAFTA (and sometimes the EU), or some measure of decisive ASEAN (or the ASEAN Secretariat) authority in ATIGA matters 'above' the Member States (based on Inama and Sim (2013a).

2015 the 'full elimination of . . . NTBs' was envisaged. Given what actions are considered, this is impossible. An agreed work programme on NTBs should have ensured that all NTBs were removed by 2010 for ASEAN-5, which did not happen and nothing specific on a work programme has been reported by ASEAN on its website until as late as 2013. ASEAN's Annual Report 2014/15 (pp. 51–2), as revised in August 2015, reports that the 'bizarre camponents of NTMs' need to be removed. What exactly this means is puzzling. The item also wants 'transparency' on NTMs, which is strange because NTMs include NTBs. Below we shall attempt to unravel the Gordian knot of NTM, NTB and SPS measures. In doing so, we shall first deal with 'core NTMs', followed by TBTs and standards. Unfortunately, SPS issues specific to ASEAN – that is, beyond or distinct from the WTO SPS Agreement and the Codex Alimentarius – cannot be surveyed as the author does not have access to the information. This is regrettable because SPS questions tend to be thorny in every regional group in the world and there is no reason to expect it to be otherwise in ASEAN. The confusion about the terms and what they mean is hopefully much reduced by Box 4.2 on classification of NTMs, including NTBs, TBTs and SPS.

For NTMs, the measures other than TBTs and SPS are often protectionist: non-automatic licensing, quantitative restrictions, prohibitions/bans, single distribution for imports and foreign exchange restrictions. They have come to be denoted as 'core NTMs'. ERIA (2012: 24) recently published data on core NTMs in ASEAN countries. Consider Table 4.1. The market failure justification of core NTMs is usually lacking or weak, or does not exist in economics. For poor ASEAN countries (e.g., Myanmar with dual exchange rates) there

Box 4.2 Classification of NTMs, NTBs, SPS measures and TBTs in the world economy

ASEAN has struggled for decades with NTMs inside ASEAN, beginning in 1987. Although this can be explained by reticence on the part of the ASEAN Member States, fearing that addressing NTMs might be too intrusive, it is also true that identification and classification issues remained a paramount and unsolved question. For the EU, with its radical 'free movement' principle and far-reaching case law (both indeed intrusive!), there is no need to classify NTMs – most such measures are forbidden anyway or must be 'justified' based on strict tests, or enjoy mutual recognition, equally based on strict CJEU case law. If justified, the EU typically seeks harmonisation, a solution hardly sought by ASEAN or not available by intent. NTMs and analogous hindrances require economic as well as legal analysis, and apparently this combination of expertise was long focused on other aspects of world trade. Lawyers turned to SPS and TBT issues in particular after the Uruguay Round, given WTO dispute settlement. In recent years, however, and after decades of neglect, there has been much greater attention paid by economists to NTMs and analogous non-tariff hindrances to cross-border trade. This was initiated inside the EU, given the strict interpretation of 'free movement of goods' and the elaborate and ever more sophisticated regime of preventing TBTs in the EU Single Market (e.g., Pelkmans 1987a; Atkins 1997; Blind 2004; Swann 2010; Correia de Brito and Pelkmans 2012), followed by some work stimulated by

Box 4.2 (cont.)

APEC (e.g., Wilson 1995). Later, this was amplified by work stimulated by several international economic institutions, resulting in a new wave of studies, such as the rich survey by WTO (2012), the work by UNCTAD and its 2006 High Level Group on NTBs (see also UNCTAD 2010), and the recent multi-agency agenda on NTMs (under the name of MAST, see, e.g., Cadot, Malouch and Saez (2012) with their toolkit for policymakers). Analytical economic work on NTMs, including case studies, is found in Cadot and Malouche (2012). It is thus hardly surprising that ASEAN felt undecided about what NTMs are and are not, what their economic impact is expected to be and how to tackle them.

In UNCTAD (2010) one finds a 'multi-agency classification on NTMs' in annex 2 (measures) and annex 3 (procedural obstacles), illustrated with many examples. This classification solves the ASEAN problem of NTM identification and classification authoritatively. The ASEAN Annual Report 2014/15 (p. 52) reports that the ASEAN database will now be aligned with the UNCTAD 2012 classification as discussed here. However, it does not solve the problem of priority setting or selection; say, a choice of what NTMs are seen as most obstructive to 'free flow' of goods or services, and addressing them first, or a selection of what ASEAN governments might consider as a necessary ingredient of the AEC programme. To get some notion of what are identified as NTMs in the classification, consider the following.

Box 4.2 (cont.)

The measures are classified in sixteen categories, some of which are familiar, such as SPS measures, TBTs, pre-shipment inspection, TRIMS and rules of origin. All these NTMs are already subject to dedicated WTO Agreements and case law of the WTO Appellate Body. Still, a close inspection of the classification strongly suggests that ASEAN could go further than these WTO Agreements in reducing the number or the restrictive impact of these NTMs. If it would do so, it would undoubtedly require credible and independent dispute settlement, since these measures are typically regulatory and demand careful judgement as has been shown decisively in the WTO. Each one of these categories is broken down into one- or two-digit classes with the (non-exhaustive) enumeration of subclasses, in fact, one has a three-digit breakdown. In these five categories, and sticking to a count of two-digit classes (or one-digit when not broken down further), the total number of distinct categories of NTMs amounts to sixty-four. Addressing these in the AEC context boils down to a huge and multi-annual programme of considerable complexity. Remember, this has to be prepared, discussed and ultimately decided in an intergovernmental setting ill-suited for such highly technical and regulatory issues, although the WTO Agreements and case law should be helpful as a foundation. The other eleven categories include price control measures (including anti-dumping and countervailing duties, but many others, too), licensing,

Box 4.2 (cont.)

prohibitions and other quantitative restrictions (including quotas and tariff rate quotas and 'voluntary export restraints'), charges, taxes and para-tariffs (including indirect taxes when levied on imports), finance measures (including bank authorisations, advance payments and multiple exchange rates), anti-competitive measures (not only, e.g., sole importing agencies, but also compulsory national insurance or transport), distribution restrictions, restrictions on post-sales service, subsidies (other than export subsidies), government procurement restrictions, intellectual property (including counterfeiting) and export-related measures (including export subsidies, export taxes and export quotas). Some of these categories are under WTO Agreements or general WTO rules, but usually only partially. The total number of distinct categories of NTMs (one- or two-digit) of these eleven categories amounts to ninety-eight. In these categories the WTO foundation is often weaker or absent, except perhaps for IPRs. Both the magnitude and the intricacy of this set of NTMs represents a major challenge to the builders of the AEC.

might sometimes be a temporary case. As we have argued, with TBTs the presumption is that there is a market failure, which, of course, ought to be verified carefully in regulatory impact assessments (RIAs) or in the underlying analysis of domestic regulatory reform. If basically justified, ASEAN countries might still enact technically different approaches – as typically happened in Europe and elsewhere – and these

Table 4.1 *Core NTMs: a crude measure of restrictiveness*

Country	Total tariff lines	Prevalence rate	Coverage rate	Core NTM restrictiveness index
Brunei	5,224	0.17	0.15	0.16
Cambodia	5,224	0.05	0.04	0.05
Indonesia	5,224	0.90	0.44	0.67
Lao PDR	5,224	0.05	0.05	0.05
Malaysia	5,224	0.61	0.42	0.52
Myanmar (A)	5,224	0.08	0.07	0.07
Myanmar (B)	5,224	0.17	0.10	0.14
Philippines	5,224	0.03	0.03	0.03
Singapore	5,224	0.04	0.04	0.04
Thailand	5,224	0.03	0.03	0.03
Vietnam	5,224	0.24	0.22	0.23

Source: ERIA (2012: 24). Prevalence rate is the number of core NTMs divided by the total number of tariff lines; coverage rate is the number of tariff lines with core NTMs as a percentage of the total number of tariff lines; the restrictiveness index is simply the average of the previous two (e.g., Indonesia with 67 per cent of lines).

disparities have to be addressed in a sound, wide-ranging and intrusive ASEAN TBT strategy. The NTMs in Table 4.1, in contrast, ought to be removed or, in a few cases only, applied in a light fashion ('proportionally'). Moreover, Narjoko (2015) shows in a business survey that the NTMs are costly for business in ASEAN. As the table shows, if free flows in goods is to be meaningful, this is urgent, even if more painful for some countries than for others.

Assuming that the more protectionist and distortive NTMs will eventually be removed, the meaning of 'free flow of goods' for business will be a function of the determination of ASEAN to remove or genuinely minimise regulatory (including technical) barriers. This will become more important the higher the level of development, since higher incomes per capita tend to induce a demand for risk-reducing regulation. Thus, the stock of domestic technical and other regulation grows steadily (with income per capita and for other reasons) and these will generate *new* regulatory barriers all the time.[1] It is therefore indispensable, if one wishes 'free flow', to devise an effective *stand-still mechanism*, combined with an AEC surveillance (based on compulsory notification) of new regulatory barriers. Item 14 mentions a commitment to 'stand-still' and even 'roll-back' for this purpose; there is a notification procedure of *new* TBTs, possibly also for 'roll-back'. Notification should, in turn, trigger consultations on the seriousness of the barriers and, sometimes, lead to joint action via standards and/or harmonisation However, this is not in the Roadmap.[2] The AFTA Council has meanwhile endorsed national and regional NTM programmes '... to identify, verify and address NTMs'. Not only is it embarrassingly late to 'identity' NTMs after decades, but it is far from clear what 'address' means. Interesting is the establishment of national 'interagency bodies' to deal with and coordinate attempts to remove NTMs as the latter are often related to domestic regulation of many kinds.

[1] I have made this point already in Pelkmans (1987a), when trying to draw lessons from the intra-EU removal of TBTs for policy-makers in ASEAN. One illustration for ASEAN today: on 29 August 2012, in *The Nation*, it was reported that the ASEAN Economic Ministers in Cambodia had expressed concerns over *rising* NTBs in the region.

[2] In ERIA (2012: 23), the mid-term review of the AEC Blueprint, it is noted that notifications of TBTs under WTO TBT obligations by ASEAN countries are often not notified to the ASEAN Secretariat.

The *removal or overcoming (via mutual recognition or harmonisation) of NTBs* has not received any systematic attention in ASEAN. It is not that ASEAN is not aware of the problem, because it had already announced common work in 1987, before AFTA was even initiated. As recently as 8 June 2013, the author retrieved the following statement from the ASEAN website: 'ASEAN Member countries have also resolved to work on the elimination of non-tariff barriers. A work programme ... is currently being finalized.'[3] Such a programme had already been announced a decade ago or even before and little seems to have happened. As far as the present author knows, there is no overall, clear strategy, or policy programme or roadmap addressing NTBs. Neither have there been economic studies[4] by ASEAN or in academia which would be helpful when beginning to address this major issue.

Before elaborating the Roadmap problems, it is probably useful to clarify terminology. NTBs is a broad category and there is little reason to distinguish them from the classification in Box 4.2. For trade in goods, by far the most important overall category is regulatory barriers, with TBTs as the largest subcategory. There are three technical barriers to trade: technical regulations; technical standards (even though they are voluntary); and conformity assessment (via testing, certification, inspection, approvals or issues of accreditation). MRAs, as encouraged by the WTO, are on conformity assessment only,

[3] Overview, AFTA, available at: www.asean.org/communities/asean-economic-community/category/overview-10.

[4] Although the McKinsey report (2003) has made a first attempt to highlight some aspects and the problems for business.

they do not alter technical regulations or standards. For resolving barriers caused by distinct technical regulations, the only ways are by harmonisation (in fact, common regulation) or mutual recognition (possible when objectives are 'equivalent', so that the technical means between two trading partners can be mutually accepted). For resolving barriers caused by distinct standards, there are no legal means since standards are voluntary by their nature. Cooperation between standard bodies may help. If a technical standard is linked to or incorporated in law, it loses its defining character, unless it is accompanied expressly by an open equivalence clause. For resolving barriers caused by conformity assessment, solutions may include an agreement not to duplicate (identical) tests, to recognise (based on certain quality criteria) one another's testing (given in standards or law), to negotiate MRAs or to harmonise conformity assessment. Since health, safety, the environment and (often) liability play a role, this domain is notoriously difficult, and removing TBTs is never fast. The sectorial scope of TBTs is vast.

In item 19 of the Roadmap, it is stated that standards and technical regulations, as well as conformity procedures, are to be harmonised 'through alignment with international practices where applicable'. Harmonisation is hardly practised outside the EU as it is demanding and presupposes similar health and safety objectives (a tall order to get that recognised). Other useful but demanding actions are stated, such as MRAs, the enhancement of technical infrastructure (also crucial for higher value-added in global value chains) and even post-market surveillance systems (which are costly). However, none of these actions is worked out in any way and hence their credibility is at least in question.

There are meanwhile a few basic documents in ASEAN preparing the ground. One important instance is the ASEAN Framework Agreement on MRAs,[5] complemented by Interpretative Notes.[6] The former essentially takes over the relevant elements of the WTO TBT Agreement and the ISO/IEC Guides related to it. Since NTBs are, more often than not, regulatory barriers, ASEAN has followed important OECD initiatives, also adopted by APEC, and written the ASEAN Good Regulatory Practices Guide.[7] The Guide is state of the art in adopting wholesale the famous OECD principles of good regulation, and includes fairly detailed specifications on RIAs recommended to be applied before legislating technical regulation.[8] If properly done – which is far from easy and is resource-intensive – it may well pre-empt many new NTBs. Of course, it does not necessarily prevent them, which means that other mechanisms in ASEAN are badly needed, irrespective of the existing NTBs. Indeed, there is seemingly no follow-up of the Guide and it is therefore everyone's guess whether regulatory quality has improved in ASEAN, which would be good for the functioning of domestic

5 See at: www.aseansec.org/6674.htm, from 1998

6 See at: www.asean.org/news/item/interpretative-notes-to-the-asean-framework-agreement-on-mutual-recognition-arrangements. A related document which largely overlaps with the two is the ASEAN Policy Guideline on standards and conformance, from 2005. However, that is precisely the Guideline for harmonisation (referred to in item 19), although it is long on principles and almost empty otherwise.

7 Endorsed by 2/40 SEOM meeting on 2–4 February 2009, in Bangkok.

8 As the European Commission has been obliged to do for every legislative proposal to Council and the European Parliament since mid-2003. The Commission writes about 100–130 RIAs per year.

markets and reduce the number of new TBTs emerging in the AEC. If new technical regulation is about to be adopted it has to be notified, just like in the WTO, to the ASEAN Secretariat under a 1998 Protocol, with a set consultation period of six months. No reports on this notification are public. The reporting under the Interpretative Notes is firmly confidential (Article 15) and so are reports to the SEOM officials. This must mean that many ASEAN TBTs are reported to the WTO while remaining unpublished in ASEAN itself.

The ASEAN Coordinating Committee on Standards and Quality (ACCSQ) was founded some time ago, but its work is not systematically published. Its policy guidelines refer frequently to the application of the principles in sectorial regulation, standards and conformity assessment issues under the 'sectorial MRAs' (for goods, not to be confused with services MRAs). However, the ASEAN website does not provide much information on these sectorial MRAs. There are MRAs in electronic goods, in cosmetics and so-called 'common technical dossiers' in medicines in preparation for marketing authorisation. One result of the ACCSQ is a list of standards for electric and electronic products and for electromagnetic compatibility (EMC)[9] (and a few for rubber-based products). This curious stand-alone list, updated since the late 1990s, contains no more than 111 standards (which is a trivial number), and practically all are international standards (IEC, ITU and specialised bodies). ASEAN national standards bodies are obliged to adopt the (voluntary) standards; if they fail to do that, there is 'direct use' of the international standard

[9] For example, interference by household equipment etc.

by the market anyway. However, even for these few well-accepted world standards, some ASEAN countries modify them or link them to regulation which might reduce flexibility for industry. World standards here are mostly product standards and can be used inside ASEAN, thereby are likely to pre-empt new NTBs while resolving a number of existing ones. Often, however, world standards are procedural or about testing or measurement and cannot pre-empt product specifications causing NTBs. Anyway, standards are in principle voluntary and it is usually technical regulations which lead to stubborn NTBs. Therefore, it is anything but clear what the meaning of the list is. This area is typically regulated in all countries and the list suggests (without saying so) that adherence to the standards is tantamount to compliance with the law. The recent work on NTBs is typically concentrated on a few priority sectors of the AEC. In a first survey of its kind, Prassetya and Intal (2015) demonstrate that all three types of TBTs (caused by standards, conformity assessment and technical regulation) are addressed to some degree in these nine sectors. However, the examples of standards are partly *not* standards at all, but technical regulations (e.g., in the car sector via UN-ECE; food regulations). This also shows that, once TBTs are addressed in earnest, forms of 'positive integration' cannot easily be avoided.

The only fully implemented instance of harmonisation of national technical regulations is the ASEAN cosmetics 'directive' (an EU term really; its text and annexes are largely adopted from EU cosmetics legislation), which seems to have brought up all the (in Europe) well-known problems of heavy-handed technical harmonisation. In case the implied risk reduction, expressed in the health and safety objectives of the regulation, is drastic, and oversight of such risks was loose and light at first, the chances are that the rules may prompt a 'raising of rivals' costs' effect vis-à-vis price fighters in the market (with indeed greater risks). Typically, such new rules tend to be supported by incumbents or by sophisticated foreign firms that are used to working with tough risk management. In Reyes' (2013) study of the implementation of the ASEAN cosmetics directive in the Philippines, this is exactly what seems to have happened. SMEs complain loudly that the costs of getting cosmetics to the market have multiplied, squeezing them out of the market or pushing them into unprofitable niches where they might survive. ASEAN faces a host of such regulatory dilemmas that, for some market players, might be about their survival if harmonisation is based on ambitious and common health, safety and environmental objectives.

Altogether, little is known about the removal or pre-emption of NTBs in the AEC, and what *is* known, is far, far too little to even begin a meaningful programme of NTB removal and/or regulatory approximation or convergence, or systematic mutual recognition. This neglect constitutes a major threat to the deepening of the AEC goods market. Furthermore, even if a programme were to be drafted soon, regulatory harmonisation under a veto system may easily lead to 'trench wars', with long delayed compromises that might well disregard 'good regulation' (Pelkmans 1987a). This is the consequence of adjustment costs in sectors (see the cosmetics example above) and the fear for industry consolidation that free market access, hitherto blocked by regulatory barriers, may bring about. By their very nature, NTBs hardly attract political attention from ministers or parliamentarians, which gives lobbyists a golden opportunity to directly influence the sectorial specialists conducting the negotiations. The more ASEAN leans on world product standards the better, but in many markets these are not available. As to regulation, mutual recognition and/or regulatory convergence in many hundreds of areas (if not more) is cumbersome. When risks for consumers or workers are relatively serious, harmonisation tends to be superior to mutual recognition. In the Roadmap there is nothing that reflects an awareness of these crucial issues for 'free flow'. A failure of ASEAN to address NTBs with gusto will throttle the beneficial market integration effects considerably.

4.1.3 Implementing the free flow of services

Free flow of services is less impressive than for goods.[10] Perhaps this is not surprising. The EU enjoys 'free movement' and extensive CJEU case law (Hatzopoulos 2012), and yet it still experiences considerable difficulties in achieving fully-fledged liberalisation of all services.[11] Even inside the United States there are a few lingering restrictions in, for example, insurance (there is no federal insurance regime, but the interstate commerce clause suppresses most incipient barriers) and interstate 'compacts' in road transport can also cause divergences between groups of US states. In any event, it is hard to escape the impression that 'free flow' of services will

[10] Financial services will be dealt with in section 4.1.5.

[11] See, e.g., European Commission (2012); Mustilli and Pelkmans (2013) for greater detail.

not be accomplished in ASEAN in 2015, or soon thereafter. Insofar as a kind of free services flow liberalisation could be achieved, it is likely to be much less ambitious than the EU internal market for services, despite the latter's incompleteness. The Roadmap idea is to liberalise modes 1 and 2 anyway, but that is accomplished via packages and rounds in AFAS. By the end of 2015 no less than eleven packages on 127 subsectors should have been completed (not including financial services and transport). In mid 2015, the ninth package was practically completed and negotiations on the tenth package had begun. Once the eleven packages are complete, the 'ultimate sectorial coverage . . . will far exceed what GATS or other FTAs entered into by ASEAN Member countries have been able to achieve so far' (Sauve, Neo and Streho 2013). Still, with the so-called 15 per cent flexibility provision under AFAS, which operates across all four modes, a considerable number of restrictions (can) remain. Moreover, the 'broad sectorial coverage . . . is not matched by a similar depth in the required commitments in terms of modes of supply' (Sauve, Neo and Streho 2013). In short, for modes 1 and 2 there will legally be a 'free flow' except for restrictions retained for bona fide regulatory reasons. However, bona fide reasons, EU experience suggests, may leave in place numerous regulatory obstacles that call for harmonisation before they could ever disappear, but this is hardly, or not, found in the Roadmap. For mode 3, it is about two key issues: equity participation of non-nationals (from ASEAN) of at least 70 per cent (in 2015), and market access obligations to be progressively liberalised, but without hard deadlines and little more than a vague promise. Mode 4 is even more problematic. The recent ASEAN Framework

Agreement for the movement of natural persons is an encouraging step. Nevertheless, 'on the ground' this has – so far – not helped in any concrete way.

As noted, the Roadmap states that there are 'No restrictions for modes 1 and 2 with exceptions due to bona fide regulatory reasons (such as public safety) which are subject to agreement by all Member Countries on a case-by-case basis'. This phrase touches the heart of the matter. Because the AEC has no 'free movement' and no central supreme court to subject national restrictions to judicial review of what goes against 'free flow' and when legitimate exceptions can be made, ASEAN has basically only two options: either one subjects each and every national law on services having restrictive effects on market access to the case-by-case review of ASEAN Member States as a group, or ASEAN decides to go for (selective) harmonisation so as to prevent such restrictive effects. Both options are bound to make ASEAN countries uncomfortable. The first option is proposed in the Roadmap, but, going by experience in the EU internal market, seems several bridges too far for ASEAN. International and intra-ASEAN trade in services is rife with restrictions that *are* justified by market failures (Dee 2005; Mustilli and Pelkmans 2013). In the EU, the much discussed 2006 Horizontal Services Directive (based essentially on free movement) covers services that tend to be relatively lightly regulated, but it took two decades of case law; a tough horizontal directive; and a special three-year 'national screening' of *all* national and regional services laws, plus a joint follow-up by member states and the Commission in a year-long 'mutual evaluation', in order to reduce significantly the numerous restrictions found.[12] It is also likely that other ASEAN Member countries will not exercise their right of veto, due to the risk that their own services laws might be blocked or stripped as well. Therefore, if this 'bona fide' clause is to be maintained, many restrictions to modes 1 and 2 might not, in fact, be removed or only made 'less restrictive'.[13]

The second option would appear *not* to be in the mindset of ASEAN decision-makers. There are a few scattered proposals for selective harmonisation (e.g., in telecoms equipment, some transport), but the indications in the Roadmap are that these would be the exceptions. A larger exception of modest 'positive integration' is found in the professional MRAs. This is a notoriously difficult area in which to accomplish 'free flow'. Eight MRAs have been signed since December 2005 including engineering, nursing, architectural services, surveying, accountancy, medical practitioners and dental practitioners. Based on Sauve, Neo and Streho (2013), we note the following. The MRAs for surveying qualifications and accountancy are in fact framework agreements facilitating later negotiations as well as information

[12] For those interested in how this special implementation was executed and how intrusive it was, see European Commission (2011). Since there are lingering doubts about the validity of some remaining restrictions (in terms of market failures), the EU will probably follow up with further attempts to narrow down the legitimate exceptions (e.g., regulated professions). See European Commission (2012).

[13] Note that the thorough screening by EU countries referred to in fn. 12, above, touched on no less than 35,000 national legal provisions. In an intergovernmental process (as ASEAN has) and without a 'mother principle' such as strict free movement, it will be next to impossible to achieve a genuine free flow with respect to modes 1 and 2, if the 'bona fide regulatory reasons' are not scrutinised by an independent body or court.

exchange. These are expected to be followed up by bilateral (or plurilateral) agreements between ASEAN countries, facilitating mobility and 'enhanc[ing] cooperation in respect of mutual recognition'. One example is found in accountancy, with the Mutual Recognition Arrangement (not Agreement, suggesting a major role of private associations in all this) being signed in November 2014. Thus, no genuine ASEAN-wide approach is foreseen, implying no level playing field and little guarantee as to what will come about. A very different approach has been taken for architects and engineers. For both, a uniquely centralised solution has been pursued in establishing two ASEAN-wide bodies endowed with the authority to confer ASEAN titles of engineer and architect.[14] This is, however, a necessary, but not a sufficient condition to operate in other ASEAN countries. Subsequently, one has to apply to become, in the relevant host country, a Registered Foreign Professional Engineer or Foreign Architect. Both MRAs have been fully implemented and countries seem to have begun to register these professionals as ASEAN professionals. The registration in ASEAN *host* countries still has to be initiated. This leaves the three MRAs in healthcare services. Although there is an ASEAN coordinating committee, there is no centralisation whatsoever, and the registration will take place on a bilateral basis. It is too early to assess whether this will actually work.[15]

[14] The ACPECC (committee) confers the title of ASEAN Chartered Professional Engineer and the AAC that of ASEAN architect.

[15] In addition, there is a MRA for tourism professionals, with an amazingly detailed regulation of no less than thirty-two job titles from front office hotel manager, via bakers to travel consultants. Although in ASEAN there might be an issue of quality so as to establish or improve a 'brand' in

In financial services, there is little clarity on the final properties of free flow. The wording is circumspect, liberalisation has a shifted deadline of 2020, not 2015 (the new approach based on 'pre-agreed flexibilities' , has been pursued in the sixth package, finished early 2015 – ambitiously incorporating elements of the ASEAN Banking Integration Framework – but it will not be signed in the routine fashion but what ASEAN calls 'ad referendum', which suggests less than full adherence for years to come), whilst being closely related with 'freer' capital flows. The negotiation of the respective packages is based on a positive list approach, which is rather prudent. Moreover, before the fifth round, negotiations were based on a request-and-offer mechanism, which equally expresses a weak impetus to liberalise. The protocol to implement the fifth package of commitments on financial services (of 4 May 2011) is a very lengthy document in which ASEAN countries typically specify the remaining restrictions in tremendous detail, both for market access and national treatment. The present monograph is not the right place to scrutinise these restrictions, but the numerous restrictions do not give much confidence that a 'free flow' of financial services will have been accomplished by late 2015 or even 2020.[16]

world tourism, there is nonetheless the question of what are the market failures that have to be overcome by such strict and encompassing micro-regulation. See Sauve, Neo and Streho (2013) for details.

[16] See at: www.asean.org/images/2012/Economic/AFMM/Agreement_on_Finance/Schedule%20of20Speific%20Commitments.pdf. For example, Malaysia uses fifty pages of small print, Indonesia twenty and the Philippines twenty-three pages.

We shall come back on the combination of financial services and free(r) capital flows, and the relation with financial stability, in section 4.2 and Chapter 5.

There is also no systematic approach to network industries. The Roadmap places them not under services, but under ASEAN infrastructure (item 2.4 in Table 3.1). The upshot is that the infrastructure part of the Roadmap blends services liberalisation with issues of 'hard' infrastructure for network industries such as telecoms, gas and electricity as well as air and maritime (and multi-modal) transport. The Roadmap speaks about an ASEAN Single Aviation Market to 'pave way for the regional "open sky" arrangement'. Such an approach does not seem coherent. A typical 'open sky' agreement goes no further than the fifth freedom (in air services rights granted), which is still quite some distance from a single aviation market. Indeed, the 2009 ASEAN Multilateral Agreement on Air Services remains somewhat open-ended (commitments only in annexes, without there being a common obligation to grant fifth freedom rights, let alone higher freedoms) and still speaks of designated airlines rather than all certified ASEAN airlines.[17] Potentially more ambitious is the Implementation Framework of the ASEAN Single Aviation Market (16 December 2012), which consists mainly of a Roadmap until 2020 or beyond. It

[17] On 12 November 2010, Protocol 1 on unlimited third and fourth freedom traffic rights was signed, which is basic given international practices, yet probably a major improvement given ASEAN's restrictive traditions in aviation. A detailed analysis of ASEAN countries' restrictive (and non-transparent) interventionism in air transport is found in Dee (2009b). The eighth package of the commitments on Air Transport Services under AFAS was signed in November 2014.

prudently states that 'the possibility of further liberalization of market access, if necessary' may be considered in the period 2016–20; referring to freight and passengers for charters, market access is only open for routes not served by scheduled services. The air Roadmap includes thirty-six action items, of which eight are beyond 2020, two are for 2016–20 and no less than fifteen are scheduled for 2015. It is therefore a typical example of the glass being half-full given past protectionism in air transport in ASEAN, the aims are commendable and will improve the business environment in terms of market integration; there is progress, surely, but the label (Single Aviation Market) is far ahead of the reality, whilst the plans are open-ended and scheduled far beyond the AEC deadline. The Roadmap also speaks of an ASEAN Maritime Shipping Market, meanwhile renamed as ASEAN Single Shipping Market, but only small steps have been undertaken so far and the implementation framework for this ASEAN shipping market was only endorsed in November 2014 by the Transport Ministers, even though it only gives 'strategic guidance' on harmonising rules to further liberalise.[18] In gas and electricity, the emphasis is almost entirely on hard infrastructure such as the ASEAN power grid and the trans-ASEAN gas pipeline. The credibility of these very costly, but potentially most useful, initiatives hinges on the private business case, given the lack of public ASEAN infrastructure funds. Of course, the business case hinges, in turn, on what ASEAN countries will allow as the function of such infrastructure, for example, filling shortages or

[18] See at: www.asean.org/images/pdf/2014_upload/20%20ATM%20JMS%20Final.pdf.

allowing peak electricity traffic only, or genuine two-way trade (at what prices?), or stronger, third-party access on interconnectors in order to stimulate competition and entry, which would be possible only under a true ASEAN market and regulatory regime. It would seem that national energy markets remain carefully separated but for peak loads and gas shortages. However, energy ministers recently agreed to conduct sub-regional electricity trading by 2018, which by definition implies forms of 'market coupling'. The term 'sub-region' presumably means bi- or tri-lateral. In ICT/telecoms – now often called eCommunications – there are MRAs on telecoms equipment (the goods segment), but little can be found on the services segment. This is clear from the 2003 Singapore Declaration, a kind of cooperative action agenda. Thus, the promotion of ICT is regarded as important, given that ICT is an 'engine for growth in ASEAN'.[19] The ASEAN ICT masterplan[20] goes a little further, but this is driven at least as much by the attractiveness of the ASEAN business environment (hence, the 'production base' aim) as by market integration. The plan speaks about a 'framework to facilitate transparent and harmonized ICT regulations' (including standards), but provides no details except the striving for common minimum standards for network security. A study on how to lower intra-ASEAN roaming charges for mobile broadband has been announced, but it should be remembered that, in the EU, this issue was resolved

[19] The title of the summary of the eleventh ASEAN telecoms ministers meeting in Myanmar, 9 December 2011.

[20] See at: www.asean.org/images/2012/Economic/TELMIN/ASEAN%20ICT%20Masterplan%202015.pdf.

only by imposing heavy-handed EU price regulation. The intention of the ASEAN telecoms regulators to lower roaming charges is apparently rather 'soft', shown by the fact that the recent agreement between Brunei and Singapore to start reducing them in 2015 is the only one, so far. Given new business models (e.g. internet based services), telecoms companies are very keen to keep roaming revenues. A link is made with IPR enforcement, another cooperative item in the AEC Roadmap. Finally, a call to develop MRAs for ICT skill certification to ensure the quality of ICT talents is probably targeted at the AEC 'production base'. Knowing what it took, and still takes, for the EU to accomplish liberalisation of network industries across intra-EU borders,[21] one wonders what the AEC in network industry services might eventually comprise.

But, as Table 3.1 shows, ASEAN has also worked on modes 3 and 4. In mode 3 (FDI or in GATS terms, commercial presence), everything turns around the allowed equity participation (aiming for a minimum of 70 per cent for all sectors in 2015). In the Roadmap this is characterised as 'substantially no restriction for establishing'. One wonders whether business investors would also see it that way. It is unclear (in the Roadmap) whether here a distinction is made between ASEAN and non-ASEAN investors in services. Finally, one wonders how the services AEC and the 'free flow of investment' can be reconciled as the Roadmap speaks of a 'free and open investment regime' by 2015. Surely, this would mean no restrictions of FDI ownership and national treatment, but the former is not attained and the

[21] See Pelkmans and Luchetta (2013); European Commission (2013), for detailed analytical surveys.

latter is conditional in services ('parameters'). On mode 4, ASEAN has moved beyond the Roadmap with the ASEAN Agreement on Movement of Natural Persons in November 2012. Although conceptually this 'freedom' matters when building an internal market, this is *a fortiori* true for world business when assessing the FDI climate and considering intra-ASEAN complementation between plants over a value chain in and around ASEAN (production base).

It is worth noting that the many packages in the liberalisation of services under AFAS are expected to be consolidated in an Agreement to be called ATISA, the ASEAN Trade in Services Agreement. This is likely to take place only after 2015. But, as is clear from a painstaking analysis by Dee (2015), for such an ATISA to be effective, much more is required, in particular a closer link with domestic regulatory services reforms and, possibly, a switch from a positive list to a negative list approach (which, in fact, is only feasible once domestic reform strategies have been carefully crafted and all major services regimes have been received first).

4.1.4 Implementing the free flow of investment

The 'free flow of investment' is crucial for both the single market and the common production base, given the developmental significance of FDI in ASEAN and the desire to continuously enhance ASEAN's position in global value chains. ASEAN is keenly aware of the much greater competition for FDI in East Asia (McKinsey 2003), and its investment regime should therefore be attractive for multinationals. The Roadmap is long on secondary policies such as FDI facilitation and joint investment promotion, but the primacy of liberalisation (which matters most for investors) is treated more cautiously. True, all ASEAN countries have meanwhile ratified ACIA (the new ASEAN Comprehensive Investment Agreement of 2009),[22] with its 'reservation lists' which should be narrowed down, if not eliminated, in steps. Basically, ACIA is both about market access and investor protection, including arbitration (hence, avoiding the non-credible ASEAN dispute settlement EDSM). The Roadmap's idea is to realise a 'free and open investment regime' with 'minimal' investment restrictions in 2015. However, the newest Scorecard (ASEAN 2012: 6) speaks of a 'free and *more* open investment regime' (emphasis added). The proof is in the eating, that is, the ACIA schedule of narrowing the 'reservation lists' in steps up until 2015 inclusive. The Roadmap characterises the three elements of liberalisation as follows. First, 'extend non-discriminatory treatment, including national treatment and MFN, to investors in ASEAN with limited exceptions, minimize and, where possible, eliminate such exceptions'. In terms of international practices, multinationals will find this a minimum condition and possibly frown upon the lack of clarity for the end goal. Second, 'reduce and, where possible, eliminate restrictions to entry for investments' in the priority goods sectors (now eight). Again, one wonders why there is no full commitment even in the priority sectors? Moreover, there is no explicit policy statement for other sectors (e.g., services). As noted above, for services, foreign equity participation is not going to be fully

[22] Combining two former Agreements, the IAI from 1998 (on liberalisation) and IGA from 1987 (on investment protection), it also enhances the approach to liberalisation somewhat and foresees some harmonisation.

liberalised in 2015. Third, an open statement without any detail in the Roadmap or its Strategic Schedule reads 'reduce and, where possible, eliminate restrictive investment measures and other impediments, including performance requirements' (presumably, TRIMs, but there is no reference to the WTO TRIMs Agreement). All this shows the critical importance of scrutinising the ACIA Schedule of narrowing the 'reservation lists' before a serious assessment can be made. A study by Urata and Ando (2009) shows that investment regimes in ASEAN countries vary greatly. Screening and appraisal especially are regarded as quite restrictive and non-transparent, and the movement of investors is impeded. Many services sectors suffer from greater protection, often out of fear of market domination by competitive foreign firms. Interestingly, although FDI restrictions do matter, a survey of Japanese investors in ASEAN done for the study found that non-legal factors would often seem to matter even more: underdevelopment, lack of transparency, ambiguity, sudden changes, frequent changes of rules and decrees, as well as uncertainty about taxation, incentives or enforcement.

Implementation problems, corruption and heavy red tape are also reported as negatively affecting the investment climate. Finally, many ASEAN countries used to rank low on the World Bank's Doing Business indicators (yet Singapore was No. 1 in 2009). Therefore, even if the reservation list of ACIA is not fully eliminated by 2015 or 2020, an improvement of all the other elements of the investment climate could no doubt greatly help to make ASEAN countries more attractive for global value chains, that is, the 'production base'. One clear example is found in business licensing, which matters for the investment climate, for which Ing and Magiera (2015)

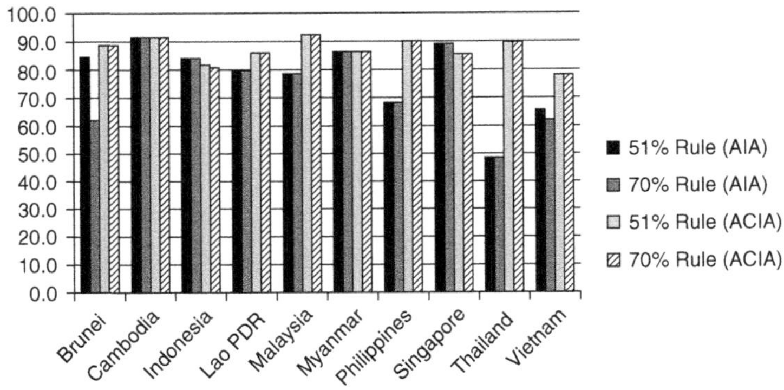

Figure 4.1 ASEAN liberalisation rates of FDI in goods sectors
Source: ERIA (2012: 14).

show how much red tape and nuisance can be removed without much effort. That 'base' does not solely depend on the measures in the Roadmap. Nevertheless, there seems to have been a recent surge in liberalisation for investment in goods sectors (key for value chains). Figure 4.1 shows a 2012 FDI liberalisation update on goods sectors composed by ERIA.

4.1.5 Implementing the free(r) flow of capital and of financial services

The 'freer flow of capital' is even more difficult to assess. The Roadmap distinguishes several components: liberalisation, harmonisation, (ASEAN) capital market development, facilitation and the closely related financial services liberalisation. It seems wise to develop an ASEAN capital market, as national equity (and bonds) markets will be too small for sufficient liquidity and depth. Nevertheless, such an initiative stands little chance of success if liberalisation of capital movements is not taken on more boldly. Prudence is driven by words like portfolio investment (and, one suspects, 'hot money', certainly after the crisis of 1997) and 'orderly capital account liberalisation'. The latter is connected with dual exchange rates (i.e., a different one for capital than that for goods and – most – services), limits on foreign exchange purchases and, for example, restrictions on repatriation of funds or proceeds. With respect to portfolio investment, for consistency with an ASEAN capital market, residents should be able to issue, purchase or sell debt securities or equity abroad – although the idea is listed, it is not clear to what extent this is going to be (fully) liberalised for a 'freer flow'. We also call attention to a few curious items. In a subsection on FDI, the Roadmap speaks about 'freer flows of FDI', which seems inconsistent with the 'free flows of investment' elsewhere, although perhaps not with the substance of the latter (see above). Under facilitation, one reads about a 'policy dialogue on prudential regulation and supervision', wording one might have expected under financial services. However, a 'dialogue' is a necessary, but far from sufficient, condition to make substantive progress. Indeed, without any harmonisation of prudential and supervision rules, it will be next to impossible to fully liberalise financial services and major distortions will remain. In this respect, readers are advised to check Annex 1 of the Roadmap (p. 66) where sixteen subsectors in financial services are identified for liberalisation in 2015. For each one of these sixteen sectors, the number of ASEAN countries is less than ten; in fact, the highest number is seven countries (re-insurance, a wholesale B2B market), and often only three or four. There is an unclear commitment about further improvements by 2020. This implies that the ASEAN 'single market' for financial services would be full of holes and distortions due to inconsistencies caused by insufficient, or no, harmonisation, as well as ever different patchworks of countries participating in each type of financial service. In fact, it would not be a single market at all.

ASEAN seems more concerned at the moment with building up a region-wide capital market in a number of ways. The development of the ASEAN bond market, its openness and liquidity is closely monitored by the Bond Market Development Scorecard. There is also an ASEAN Corporate Governance Scorecard for listed companies, as well as the development of ASEAN Disclosure Standards, early elements required to arrive at an integrated ASEAN capital market with similar regulatory ambitions underlying the confidence of investors.

Moving on disclosure standards is done in a very prudent fashion: in May 2015, a Memorandum of Understanding to establish the Streamlined Review Framework for the ASEAN Common Prospectus was signed, but only by three countries (Malaysia, Singapore, Thailand).

Financial services represents yet another example where the AEC Roadmap says rather little, other than 'pre-agreed flexibilities' (i.e., retained restrictions). As Table 2.1 notes, five liberalisation packages have been accomplished, but merely on uninteresting items. Recalling Annex 1 to the Roadmap, specifying what market or financial activities can be liberalised by 2015, the ambition is low and heterogeneity between ASEAN countries is worrying. The sixth package of financial services liberalisation has been signed early 2015. This package is more ambitious in that it is linked with the approval of the ASEAN Banking Integration Framework (in December 2014). Under this Framework, any two ASEAN countries may enter into reciprocal bilateral agreements to provide Qualified ASEAN Banks (QABs), with greater market access and other specifications consistent with domestic banks in the two countries. This may mean that deeper commitments are finally losing their taboo status. Indeed things may have changed as a designated Roadmap for Monetary and Financial Integration of ASEAN has been elaborated. Why so late? There are several reasons why the delay is understandable. First, ASEAN is small in financial terms, irrespective of whether one looks at the size of ASEAN banks or the depth and liquidity of national financial markets. Although this suggests a case for market integration, it is a far bolder step for ASEAN to do this than it was for mature markets and big players in the EU. Second, ASEAN countries needed time to improve the efficiency and soundness of their financial institutions after the East Asian financial crisis, while at the same time developing their money and capital markets. Third, financial services integration in a 'single-market-minus' cannot be dealt with without careful consideration of capital account liberalisation, quite an issue for developing countries. Both the second and the third argument are intimately linked with the possibility of incurring systemic risks and contagion, in other words, with financial stability, the loss of which could be very damaging for economic growth for several years. It goes without saying that the recent global financial crisis has served as a major warning for ASEAN countries that the design of such a single-market-minus in financial services must be sound and robust, whilst leaving some discretion in the margin for countries to act (restrictively) in the presence of financial turbulence. A recent summary report[23] has finally clarified how ASEAN regards the road to financial market integration, and it is interesting to mention a few highlights. This report consolidates the AEC Roadmap (strategic schedule), the Roadmap for Monetary and Financial Integration of ASEAN and the banking sector masterplans of ASEAN countries. The starting point is a two-speed approach for the ASEAN-5 and the other countries. It defines the market as financially integrated once participants face a single set of rules, have equal access and receive equal treatment. This is rather ambitious indeed. Stimulated by APEC and the G-20 debates, the report suggests proceeding with no less than six initiatives, which all makes sense but which is pretty daunting given where ASEAN comes from and knowing the hesitations of the group. They include: (i) greater ASEAN-wide liquidity support beyond the Chiang-Mai initiative (which has, so far, never been activated); (ii) reforming the financial sector for more adequate service; (iii) an ASEAN-wide early-warning system (presumably about systemic risks); (iv) harmonising the regulatory systems of ASEAN countries; (v) a framework for cross-border resolution for banks; and (vi) an emphasis on building common ASEAN financial institutions promoting 'orderly' integration. This list is amazingly courageous. Read against the backdrop of the reticence in the AEC Roadmap to go deep in many instances, these intentions seem coherent and appropriate. But, of course, it is one thing to write a consistent and sensible report and quite another to travel the long and

[23] ADB/ASEAN (2013)

winding road to the end goal. Thus, at the moment, banking regulation and licensing in ASEAN countries de facto still discriminate against ASEAN banks because they impose a 'needs test' which practically excludes local banks in the region from establishing themselves in other ASEAN countries.[24] It would go beyond the scope of this monograph to discuss the details of the plan for harmonisation.[25]

Economists expect the integrated banking market to reduce banking costs in the region, mobilise more savings, allocate these to more productive investment and hence increase total factor productivity, leading to higher growth. There should also be greater resilience as along as possible contagion effects can be nipped in the bud or pre-empted. The study suggests that, by 2020, the financial AEC could be 'semi-integrated'. It would introduce the notion of QABs, once core regulatory conditions could be proven to be fulfilled. Meanwhile, as noted before, a first step has been made with the ASEAN Banking Integration Framework. It would have to be accompanied by capital account liberalisation, the economic case being similar to banking integration, with the important addition of greater liquidity in the ASEAN capital markets. This is, rightly, seen as sensitive, given the macro-economic risks, financial stability risks and a risk of capital flow reversal. These risks suggest a particular sequencing, which gets much attention in the study. Common and national safeguards need to be in place. As to monitoring, the report

[24] One condition is often that the bank must be amongst the top 200 banks in the world.

[25] On entry and licensing, capital requirements of banks, supervision standards, empowerment of supervisors to take prompt corrective action, a regime of risk management procedures and transparency.

suggests a combination of the ASEAN Secretariat and an entirely new organisation. Finally, there are detailed proposals for an ASEAN payments system. With so many initiatives, some legislative, other ones 'soft' law, other ones mere intentions, plans, incentives or scorecards, it is difficult to obtain a clear view of where ASEAN is going with respect to financial integration.[26] Some modest initiatives have been undertaken such as the doubling of the Chiang-Mai swaps to US$240 billion, an ASEAN Capital Market Infrastructure Blueprint aiming to realise full access to one another's capital markets (including the nexus of clearing settlement and custody), deepening insurance integration (by a committee of ASEAN regulators), (a few) common guarantees for the issuance of infrastructure bonds and the elevation of the ASEAN-plus-three Macro-economic Research Office (AMRO) into as international organisation. However, there is also the fact of a two or multi-speed financial or capital market integration for a long time to come.

4.1.6 Implementing other free flows

The free flow of skilled labour comprises the practical facilitation of the intra-ASEAN movement of business persons, including professionals and skilled labour (visas and employment passes) so crucial for the lubrication of intra-ASEAN segments of value chains. Moreover, it seeks increased mobility for students and staff of ASEAN universities and two complementary approaches to mutual recognition of professionals' competences. The latter consists of the eight MRAs

[26] For a similar view, see Wihardja (2014).

discussed above, on the one hand, and voluntary cooperation on what is called 'concordance of skills and qualifications' for all services sectors, on the other. Both are cumbersome to pursue, but the latter can only be interpreted as a very long-term policy, far beyond the AEC deadline. Nowhere in the Roadmap is there an indication that market access to national (skilled) labour markets will be 'free'. Thus, one might query what the terms of employment passes are; are they automatically renewed, how do skilled workers from other ASEAN countries fit the local social policies, are they to be insured, are there implicit or explicit quotas, etc. As noted, the ASEAN Agreement on Movement of Natural Persons (MNP) was signed in 2012. This is strictly a 'mode 4' agreement, that is, for temporary provision of services in another ASEAN country. It refers to, for example, business visitors, contractual service suppliers and intra-corporate transferees. However, the Agreement is mainly procedural and 'nothing in the MNP Agreement requires Member States to make any further substantive commitments to liberalise Mode 4' (Sauve, Neo and Streho 2013), although there is an obligation on the countries to initiate discussions with a view to improve their schedules of commitments. Altogether, the term 'free flow of skilled labour' would seem to be a rather sunny view of what can be achieved here.[27] One suspects that this segment of the Roadmap has much more to do with the lubrication of intra-ASEAN production networks and their suppliers, be they in goods or in services, a matter of vital interest to ASEAN. Sauve, Neo and Streho (2013) point out that this eventual

[27] See also Chia (2014).

temporary entry liberalisation is carefully segregated from the MRAs of professionals. This is done by setting criteria for business persons etc. that cannot be easily fulfilled by such professionals (e.g., the remuneration of the temporary work has to come from the host country). Thus, the MRAs for professionals are really for those seeking permanent employment or establishment in another ASEAN country, not for temporary service provision.

4.2 Implementing the AEC's single market

The second query in section 3.3 is about the ASEAN single market. Table 3.1 and the analysis of 'free(r) flows' in section 4.1 essentially confirm that ASEAN will *not* get a single market in the sense of internationally agreed characteristics or stage 6 of Table 2.1. Of course, this statement is perfectly compatible with the observation that, over a wide spectrum of areas relevant for the ASEAN single market, progress has been made and in some domains indeed significant progress. Remember that stage 5 of Table 2.1 (a common market) would require fundamental 'negative integration' obligations which ensure free market access in goods, services, labour, capital and codified technology, in combination with the necessary positive integration. Such fundamental obligations have not been codified, let alone ratified, in ASEAN. Our analysis of the Roadmap and its current practical follow-up clearly shows, for each one of these five types of markets, that such free market access is most unlikely to be achieved as fully as this stage requires. The AEC would therefore seem to approximate a kind of stage 4 in Table 2.1. Table 3.1 shows that ASEAN does occasionally revert to instances of positive integration, but only very selectively, whilst staying clear of setting up credible common institutions and hard rules in order to ensure proper implementation and enforcement. One observes a slight relaxation of this ASEAN attitude during the intense build-up of the AEC. Positive integration has become more acceptable in that a few instances of harmonisation have been approved and a few more are foreseen, and some attempts to set common standards are undertaken. There is also a political recognition in declarations about the post-2015 AEC work that ASEAN institutions be strengthened and better implementation be accomplished, also with a stricter and detailed monitoring. Especially in the goods, services and labour markets where market failures have to be overcome, the lack of common institutions, the frequent absence of minimum regulatory requirements, of (sometimes) detailed common regulation (e.g., in SPS regulation, financial services, many forms of risk regulation for goods and services, network services, etc.) and of far too few common standards, amounts to an impossible hurdle for achieving a truly single market with unimpeded flows and minimal distortions. A similar conclusion follows from employing the pure economic criterion of price convergence – ASEAN will not in and by itself generate similar prices. Such price convergence would require unhindered competitive pressures throughout ASEAN based on actual and potential cross-border rivalry in all markets, given very low trading costs, options for arbitrage and easy market access, whether via trade, FDI or licensing.

The harder question to answer is what the '*sui generis*' form of a single market ASEAN-style would eventually be? This query will be taken up in Chapter 6 by considering various options. Some first reflections can be provided here given the discussion of the Roadmap. Going by Table 3.1 for the moment, access to each other's goods markets will be much freer than under AFTA, but the great challenge will consist in the removal of NTMs and a long-term programme of (mostly technical) harmonisation, MRAs and technical standards, which will enable the actual costs (of these impediments, even when justified by risk regulation) of market access to be cut drastically. In NAFTA, a FTA-plus, this is a problem, too, but its economic significance is likely to be much lower in many goods markets due to the fact that a lot of technical standards have been voluntarily written by Canada and the United States together for decades, and it is attractive (and easy) for Mexico to adopt those as well. This has everything to do with the huge economic dominance of the US market for trade and FDI in Canada and Mexico. Only in highly regulated markets, often with independent regulatory authorities, does NAFTA experience severe access costs because there is no harmonisation.

In services, the AEC picture is hard to 'read'. In 2015, it would seem to remain incomplete in a number of ways, and harmonisation as well as institutional issues are so ill-defined at the moment that it is too early for a reliable assessment. Modes 1 and 2 may well be liberalised fully, but this does not mean that no legitimate regulatory barriers will remain. A great tolerance for such lingering barriers is a practical way out for the AEC, but this will, of course, erode the single market idea. Knowing what the Roadmap says on modes 3 and 4, the outcome might be geared to what value chains and related activities need, without much ado on the single market concept. In financial services, it seemed at first doubtful whether ASEAN wanted any single market at all but, as elaborated in section 4.1.5, ASEAN had articulated a greater ambition by 2013.

When it comes to free investment flows and 'freer' capital flows, the first intention of ASEAN is more ambitious than the second. Nevertheless, it is puzzling when taking into account the developmental significance of FDI and the emphasis on hooking up with global value chains that the foreseen investment regime is only slowly improving and in the final analysis still remains somewhat restrictive. To appreciate the link with the global value chains it is useful to focus solely on the goods sectors (see Figure 4.1).

In addition, one can pose the question whether part 2 of the Roadmap ('competitive economic region') should be taken into account for the appreciation of the ASEAN single market. In a fully-fledged single market (as the EU almost is), competition policy, consumer protection and IPRs are the subject of positive integration. That is, in the EU there is a common (and forceful) competition policy, considerable harmonisation of consumer protection is pursued and IPRs are regulated and enforced at the EU level.[28] But items 2.1–2.3 in

[28] The EU has had five decades (since 1962) of resistance to a common EU patent regime, almost entirely due to the veto system (a rare exception nowadays in Brussels). Other IPRs such as trademarks, copyright, neighbouring rights, designs, are all EU regulated and EU trademarks are granted by a central agency. The EU patent is finally emerging (but for twenty-five rather than twenty-eight EU countries). The new EU patent, under the title Unitary Patent, and its common enforcement regime, came into force in 2014.

Table 3.1 are all about *national* regulation, except for the rapid alert on unsafe products. There is no intention to harmonise anywhere, although 'soft' cooperation, policy 'emulation' and dissemination of 'best practices' are pursued. Lee and Fukunaga (2013) find that the intra-ASEAN cooperation in developing and spreading competition policies has been quite intense. At the same time, only five countries have introduced competition policies and some only very recently. In other words, ASEAN may well become a better marketplace – say, for attracting FDI – when all ASEAN countries have developed these cooperative policies and regulations, but this will not contribute to the single market. Indeed, although it is early days, ASEAN may miss an opportunity to harmonise when it is still easy to do, namely, when several countries do not yet have a mature regulatory regime with vested interests. Stimulating more developed national regulatory regimes risks the emergence of new intra-ASEAN barriers in the medium term. In item 2.5 of the Roadmap there is a call to complete the network of taxation bilaterals (avoiding double taxation) in ASEAN, a small but useful ingredient of the undistorted and 'free investment flows' in the envisaged single market. Overall, the competitive economic region part in the Roadmap may be useful for the single market in only a few instances. The expected effects of national competition policies for the 'competitiveness' of ASEAN should not be exaggerated, unless they substitute a prior regime of privileges and (distribution?) monopolies. In a comparison of four national competition policies by Pupphaseva *et al.* (2009), it is not only found that there are quite a few exceptions to the application of anti-trust, but also that those four ASEAN countries differ considerably in what is covered as well as what areas fall under exceptions.[29] For the single market what matters is, first, whether restrictive business practices de facto impede market access,[30] and, subsequently, whether efficiency is effectively stimulated. Good IPR regimes in ASEAN countries are primarily of interest as another attractive element to lure world investors, besides creating more incentives for innovation.

Finally, the *sui generis* ASEAN-style single market is not easy to comprehend if one turns to the external dimension. The root of the problem is the underlying FTA status of the AEC. An FTA leaves in place the national autonomy for FTA countries for trade (and investment) policy vis-à-vis third countries. Thus, if the individual FTA countries go out into the world and conclude bilateral FTAs with individual non-FTA trading partners, this is what one should expect. In other words, AFTA and individual bilaterals with non-ASEAN countries are legally compatible and conceptually acceptable. However, once serious commitments are made (in summits, a charter and formal agreements on a range of specific issues) to construct a single market, this individual country autonomy to conclude bilaterals with outsiders sits at least uncomfortably with the common pursuit, if not worse. Today, some ASEAN countries have agreed in a binding fashion to honour forms of

[29] There is more descriptive detail about national competition policies in Lee and Fukunaga (2013), but the authors refrain from a critical analysis.

[30] Thus, although Pupphavesa *et al.* (2009) are very critical about, for example, transport restrictions and protection at national level, the transport sector seems not to be exempted from anti-trust in the four countries. This is likely to be inconsistent (or points to an error in their comparison).

liberalisation in trade in goods, services and investment with one or the other non-ASEAN country that the same ASEAN country does not (yet) concede inside ASEAN. Even if one accepts that the term 'single' for the AEC should be understood in a more pragmatic way, there can be no doubt that unconditional discretion for ASEAN countries to practise independent trade policies vis-à-vis the rest of the world will further undermine the notion of more or less homogeneous market access characteristics. It is also bound to create distortions and might generate complicated problems inside the region.

This has been realised – although a little late – and the Roadmap therefore states that 'ASEAN shall work towards maintaining "ASEAN centrality" in its external economic relations' (in 4.1 of Table 3.1), 'possibly arriving at common approaches.' A similar issue is the disparities in MFN tariffs for third countries, which may be as high as 30 per cent or more precisely amongst the relatively few tariffs which are still high. Again, this is bound to create incentives for trade deflection, which, in turn, might prompt customs to keep more cumbersome controls than would otherwise be the case. In fairness, despite ASEAN being an FTA, it has recently demonstrated an amazing capacity to conclude common framework FTAs with a range of important trading partners such as Japan, China, Korea, India and Australia/New Zealand. These framework FTAs do not go very deep, but are often made more binding in follow-up FTAs with individual ASEAN countries.[31] The ASEAN attempt to conclude a framework FTA with the EU

[31] See Cremona *et al.* (2013) for a very detailed survey of all FTAs ASEAN has concluded, including a typology.

foundered in 2008/9, among other reasons[32] because the EU policy is to conclude 'deep and comprehensive' FTAs. ASEAN has also pursued a step-by-step approach, with follow-up agreements to the framework FTAs on specific, more difficult issues (e.g., investment). Last, but not least, ASEAN has assumed leadership in pushing for 'convergence' of all FTAs with East Asian countries in the Regional Comprehensive Economic Partnership (RCEP) initiative, initiated in November 2012. By 2015, RCEP had concluded its fifth round of negotiations and it was held officially that it would be accomplished by late 2015. Given the competitive regionalism with TPP and TTIP, the RECP is likely to be more ambitious than originally foreseen and significantly reduce the inconsistencies with ASEAN's intended single market. It is the RCEP which is the result of the emphasis on 'ASEAN centrality'. This frantic FTA activity at ASEAN level tends to reduce the inconsistencies for the single market flowing from the lack of a common trade policy.

4.3 Implementing 'ASEAN as a production base'

This brings us to the third question asked in section 3.3: ASEAN as a production base. In the Roadmap there is practically no

[32] And because the EU was not prepared to negotiate with Myanmar unless and until the regime changed and respected human rights, while extending basic political freedoms to the Myanmar population. Since mid-2012 the EU has shifted markedly in lifting sanctions and restored more friendly relations, given the changes in Myanmar. The EU is now negotiating with four ASEAN countries separately (Singapore already concluded), but has not given up negotiating a framework agreement at a later stage.

explicit reference to the production base. Yet it might well be the more important AEC agenda in the minds of ASEAN leaders. Here and there, the production base is explicitly referred to the reform of the origin rules 'to respond to changes in global production processes', and a soft cooperative approach (best practices and standards in production and distribution) in D.2 under the subtitle 'enhanced participation in global supply networks'. The failure to articulate a clear and focused agenda for production networks might be seen as confirming our view that it is difficult, and perhaps even undesirable, to separate the single market and the production base. But, of course, many elements in the Roadmap have been incorporated just as much for the production base as for the single market. We mention the more important ones: the removal of NTMs; ASEAN cumulation of rules of origin (ROO); ASEAN 'authorised traders'; the modernisation of customs (eCustoms, similar documents, etc.); Single Window; ASEAN cargo processing; ASEAN Customs Transit; selective standardisation (e.g., telecoms equipment and parts, electric and electronic inputs); selective MRAs in goods; selective MRAs for professionals in services; the ACIA; better IPRs in ASEAN countries; various transport agreements (air freight, air travel, shipping); avoidance of double taxation; ASEAN infrastructure initiatives; and, finally, greater coherence in ASEAN's external economic relations, in particular, nationally concluded FTAs with non-ASEAN countries. All these items can just as well be seen as building blocks of the single market.

It is therefore arbitrary, if not mistaken, to single out one or other policy domain and assert that it is, or would be, central to the ASEAN production base, but irrelevant to the single market. Rather, it is usually a question of 'direct or indirect'. In any event, the Roadmap does not provide hints about a 'conceptual' approach to the production base. In section 3.3 we attempted to provide an economic underpinning of the ASEAN production base for the purpose of attracting more and higher value-added segments of global value chains. The policy conclusions of this analysis are utilised in Chapter 6 on the future options for the AEC.

At this stage, we shall nevertheless single out two policy domains that might be regarded as more directly relevant for the production base than for the single market: the transaction costs of customs for international business; and ASEAN cross-border infrastructure. As to the former, for the single market, equal treatment and conformity with agreed ASEAN procedures for customs are obviously paramount. Although this matters, of course, for the production base as well, when assessing the customs from the point of view of business engaged in multi-country value chains, the actual transaction costs of passing customs are much more important. ASEAN exhibits huge differences on the latter, ranging from four days in Singapore to forty-five days in Lao. There are also nuisance costs to delays, other than the number of days. Cutting the number of days for goods lingering in customs is therefore a priority for business and even more in global value chains.

There is also a range of other customs issues that matter a great deal for companies (cf. Inama and Sim 2013a, 2013b). That is why the business opinion on *actual implementation* of the ASEAN customs programmes matters so much. Figure 4.2 tells a mixed story, but there seems to be considerable progress in the ASEAN-5 countries.

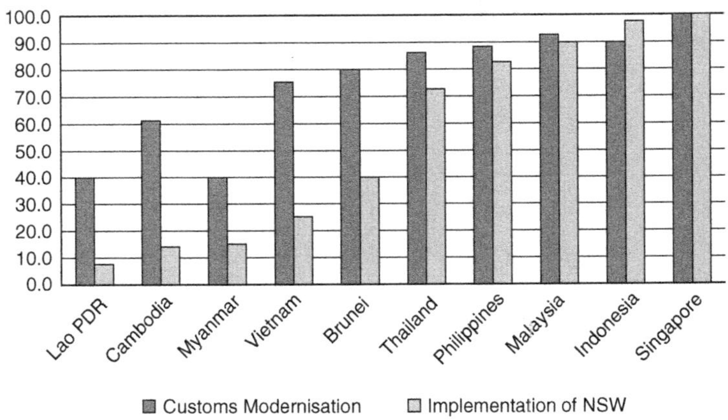

Figure 4.2 ASEAN business scores on customs modernisation and the Single Window

ASEAN infrastructure (2.4 in the Roadmap), if effectively built up, is of course of great importance for the cost reduction of logistics (one of the biggest problems of both domestic *and* intra-ASEAN trade), and for the quality and availability of energy and, for example, broadband. Connectivity in physical transport and via electronic and energy networks in ASEAN still leaves much to be desired. It would not be surprising to find that infrastructural improvements for the region as a whole may do more to lower costs than the removal of low tariffs and even the removal of NTMs. Indeed, a simulation by ERIA (2012) of the economic impact of transport infrastructure investments and specific facilitation measures yields an increment to the 2010 ASEAN GDP of no less than 13 per cent, with CMLV, Indonesia and the Philippines enjoying the highest positive impact of up to 20 per cent or even more. Such dramatic GNP gains may sound implausible. However, as an archipelago that has long underinvested in connecting infrastructure, perhaps such large effects are not entirely surprising. The question is, however, what the incentives are for ASEAN countries to invest heavily in these initiatives.[33] There is also no common public fund. The new ASEAN Infrastructure Fund (linked to bond markets, and hence to private money, see 1.4 of the Roadmap) might be of concrete help here. However, the present capital of not even €500 million seems to severely limit the possibilities to undertake meaningful infrastructure projects on an ASEAN scale.

As far as the present author knows, ASEAN has never assessed whether there is enough progress in nearing the goal of making ASEAN a better 'production base'. Admittedly, this would require defining in operational terms what ASEAN would see as the minimum set of improvements in liberalisation, regulation and ASEAN, as well as national policies for the region to serve as a better 'base'. This has not been done. Although one might argue that it has also not been done for the single market, there is a widespread understanding that free and open market access inside ASEAN is a condition *sine qua non* for the single market, to be achieved via some combination of negative and positive integration. How far one might get in moving up to higher stages (in Table 2.1) such as stages 4, 5 or 6 is complex, but the general idea is clear.

[33] Pupphavesa *et al.* (2009: 69–72) report resistance and a lack of political will due to entrenched protectionism in, for example, most transport modes in ASEAN.

For the production base, a defining idea is lacking. Based on some economic reflections in section 3.3.3, we shall attempt to formulate policy implications for the ASEAN production base and utilise these for the options in Chapter 6.

Chapter 5

A reality check: comparing the AEC and NAFTA on substance

After comparing the AEC and NAFTA with respect to design (in section 2.4), the elaborate analysis of the expected and realised substance of the AEC until mid-2013 in this chapter provides a basis for a comparison with NAFTA on the substance of implementation. The AEC and NAFTA share several characteristics when it comes to substance, although this is rarely emphasised. Put differently, the substance of NAFTA does not seem overly ambitious for ASEAN when assessed against the backdrop of the emerging AEC. The most important difference is, of course, that NAFTA does not pretend to form a single market. However, if one studies the substantive building blocks, the two regional integration attempts are fairly similar. In order to clarify this point, Table 5.1 sums up the substance of NAFTA in the first two columns, with some comments in the third. The fourth column indicates whether the AEC has, or may have, similar provisions, and the fifth column stylises the EU regime in the same domain merely for comparison.

Table 5.1 summarises practically all the substantive provisions of NAFTA in fifteen horizontal or vertical domains (and the two side agreements on labour and environment). It is recommended that NAFTA should be evaluated against the backdrop of the Uruguay Round and the resulting Marrakesh

Table 5.1 *Substantive design of NAFTA compared with the AEC and the EU*

Subject areas	Key provisions NAFTA	Comments	AEC	EU
1. Tariffs	Industrial FTA; selective liberalisation of agriculture.	Done.	Some exclusion still; export taxes a rising issue; some disparities MFN tariffs.	Zero and intra-EU free (CU) circulation.
2. Market access in goods				
2.1 Cars	Free intra-trade; restrictive origin rules.	See 3.	Almost free, liberal origin; cars not free; temporary issues.	Free, semi-liberal origin, free.
2.2 Textiles/cloth	Free intra-trade; restrictive origin rules; safeguards; tariff rate quotas; labelling.	See various, below	Restrictive investment rules, chemicals.	Free, no investment rules; no ownership restrictions.
2.3 Energy	Conditionally free intra-trade (licences possible), also for derived products (petrochemicals); investment rules; ownership restrictions.	WTO-based rules, plus specifics,	Problems in rice and sugar; no export subsidies; domestic support mixed.	Free intra-EU; high outside tariffs in some agro-goods; income subsidies.
2.4 Agriculture	In fact, three bilateral agreements; considerable liberalisation; explicit trade diversion in sugar; restrictions, safeguards; WTO-inspired rules on domestic	complicated.		

	support; export subsidies and marketing.			
3. Origin rules	Basics: change in tariff classification (=substantial transformation) in goods for NAFTA origin; restrictive rules for textiles and clothing (yarn forward, fibre forward) and cars (62.5 or 60 per cent), TVs, semi-conductors, some agriculture; customs valuation as WTO code.	The sectoral rules are so restrictive that they may magnify trade diversion (hence, violate Article 24 GATT)	AEC has several origin rules, also the NAFTA rule.	EU has several origin rules, and Europe-wide cumulation (beyond EU).
4. Safeguards	Bilateral and 'global'(WTO) safeguards.	Against intra-NAFTA import surges; automatic phase-out.	Simple safeguards in AFTA (withdrawals).	None
5. Harmonisation		Very modest, very selective	AEC now on similar track of modest harmonisation, also relies on MRAs.	EU harmonises (regulates) when market failures or disparities sufficiently distortive; now thousands of EU laws for goods, services, plus 25,000 European standards.
5.1 Safety	Consensus-based processes on transport Safety standards	(incl. UN-based norms for		

Table 5.1 (*cont.*)

Subject areas	Key provisions NAFTA	Comments	AEC	EU
		hazardous materials); such as the WTO SPS Code (signed 1994).		
5.2 Public health/ phytosanitary	Only reference to international standards; inquiry points; basic principles.			
6. Customs	Incentives for some harmonisation (certificate of origin); phase-out of (intra-NAFTA) drawbacks and user fees.		AEC customs issues, many, but being addressed.	EU = a CU, all customs rules plus documentation identical; no intra-EU frontiers.
7. Services/general	Liberalisation (production, distribution, sale, use, etc.); national treatment; no local presence requirement (with many exceptions); basic principles for licensing and certification.	A kind of GATS with more direct market access; more key for investment than trade in services, effects not so clear, sectoral exceptions.	AEC slow in services, but in principle, modes 1 and 2 free soon (except financial services); network sectors unclear; modes 3 and 4 harder.	Non-discrimination plus national treatment; fully free intra-EU trade in all modes; licensing discouraged; has to strictly guarantee non-discrimination.
8. Services/specific				
8.1 Financial	MFN and national treatment; still major national discretion (prudential rules, pensions); only	In practice, it is Mexico opening up (with safeguards),	Problematic in AEC; little progress, uneven between countries and services.	Fully free integrated markets; supervision EU rules; national bodies (shifts to

	procedural harmonisation (information etc.)	mainly investment-driven (see 8.1).		EU now); EU prudential rules, also insurance; EU regulates telecoms; mixed competition policy, etc. free; no misleading adverts (EU); intra-EU transport free; EU safety regulation (air, rail, maritime).
8.2 Insurance	Some extra transition provisions.	Close to WTO telecoms agreement (e.g., reference doc.).	So far hardly addressed.	
8.3 Telecoms	Fairly basic WTO-based package, removing only highly restrictive or discriminatory practices.		Most ASEAN id.	
8.4 Advertising	National treatment.		Not yet addressed. AEC transport policy beginning (air seems a little more liberal).	
8.5 Transport	Trucking, bus, rail and port services plus related services (even pipelines); free access, subject to (sometimes) licences or certificates; no cabotage; no foreign ownership of domestic providers.	Modest liberalisation, but suitable to facilitate free goods trade.		

Table 5.1 (*cont.*)

Subject areas	Key provisions NAFTA	Comments	AEC	EU
9. Intellectual property	Basically, the TRIPs agreement *avant la lettre*, and to execute Geneva, Berne, Paris and plants conventions.		AEC merely light IPR cooperation.	IPRs mostly EU, where national, rules are harmonised.
10. Investment				
10.1 General	National treatment; MFN; no performance requirements; free transfers (convertible currency); expropriations (plus compensation) rules (with exceptions).	Beyond TRIMs and close to OECD codes.	AEC vows to follow these norms, yet hesitant and selective.	Idem. to NAFTA, but EU-wide (based on a right) and no exceptions.
10.2 Transport	Foreign ownership only for cross-border service providers; specific sectoral ownership restrictions (e.g., ports, airlines).		AEC for ASEAN owners of transport providers, progress slow.	No restrictions.
11. Government procurement	Only for federal government; just few 'Buy American' restrictions lifted.	Revision(?) with (plurilateral) WTO code (see 13).	No AEC provisions.	Strict EU public procurement procedures, all levels; EU-wide notification beyond (low) thresholds.

12. Trade remedies	No anti-dumping, or countervailing duties or harmonisation at all; is basically about dispute settlement.				Intra-EU no trade policies left.
13. Dispute settlement					
13.1 General	Binding (binational) panel rulings, no appeal; panel composition from rosters; strict deadlines.		EDSM Charter.		EU has no 'dispute settlement', as there is no dispute between EU countries, a country can 'infringe EU law' and the Commission or the CJEU enforce.
13.2 Anti-dumping	No prior consultation; panel selection problematic; limited private standing;	Note: US national rules problematic; most cases in this area. No punitive damages (in US law, common).			
13.3 Investment	Staged approach: first, bilateral conciliation attempt, then arbitration (panel of three, ICSID as last resort).		ACIA and other progress on investment protection.		

Table 5.1 *(cont.)*

Subject areas	Key provisions NAFTA	Comments	AEC	EU
14. Anti-trust	Requirement for NAFTA member states to have a competition policy; cooperation on anti-trust themes is very soft; state enterprises cannot discriminate, but otherwise free; even certain monopolies can stay.	No cross-border provisions whatsoever.	Only call to have national competition policy, based on handbook.	Fully-fledged and credible EU and national competition policies.
15. Temporary entry	Facilitation, categories of business persons identified; no change or immigration, security or employment policy; no dispute settlement.	Categories of business executives (e.g., in MNCs), and in professional services.	ASEAN Agreement on Movement of Natural Persons (see section 4.1.6 in text).	Fully free intra-EU movement of all workers or any persons; migrants plus temporary providers paid local wages.
16. Side agreements	In labour and environment.	Was political condition in the US.		Part of EU regulation.

Agreements of GATT/WTO, which six ASEAN countries have signed. NAFTA was negotiated before Marrakesh (1994), but the drafting of NAFTA's substance was simultaneous with the deliberations in Geneva on draft texts in, say, 1991–1993. NAFTA was also greatly influenced by the FTA between Canada and the United States concluded in 1989. Seen in this light, NAFTA is not a sensationally 'deep' FTA. As one can quickly derive from Table 5.1, NAFTA is a kind of '*regionalised WTO-plus*'.

This regionalised WTO-plus is characterised by both deepening of WTO commitments and some widening (beyond the scope of WTO disciplines). *Deepening* is found in tariff removal of the FTA[1] in agriculture (where GATT/WTO does not yet go very far); in selective harmonisation (modest, now that the SPS agreement works); and in services (where GATS has similar principles, but with more remaining discretion for national governments and open-ended – in actual practice, disappointing – lists of commitments to open up; whereas in NAFTA the specifics are technical, yet, on the whole as well as in the sectors specified, they go further

[1] Ever since the theory of preferential trading has been around, it has been well known that an FTA (and not only a CU) can cause trade diversion, hence, it cannot be regarded as a pure move towards free trade, that is, a pure deepening of WTO tariff concessions. NAFTA is likely to cause trade diversion where tariff disparities are high and/or where origin rules are restrictive. In addition, there are agricultural provisions, for example, in sugar, where explicit requirements have been incorporated that impose a joint discrimination of third countries' suppliers, which, by definition, will augment trade diversion. All in all, tariff removal in the FTA is deepening, but the effects need not necessarily be beneficial to third partners and/or for economic welfare.

and are pre-committed, hence, give legal certainty for competitive strategies).

Widening of scope beyond what the WTO currently covers is also achieved by NAFTA. The carefully circumscribed harmonisation in customs and transport, the rules on investment (and by implication, the dispute settlement on investment), those on government procurement (here, there is a so-called 'plurilateral' code, agreed after NAFTA; a plurilateral code is negotiated in the framework of WTO, but only obligatory for the signatories, that is, not part of the 'single package' of the Uruguay Round), dispute settlement on anti-dumping and countervailing duties (remember, a unique discipline for the United States without appeal), anti-trust cooperation even if soft, and finally the facilitation of temporary entry for business persons and professionals.

It would thus be mistaken to regard NAFTA as a very 'deep' form of market integration. In terms of Table 2.1, it hangs between stage 3 and 4. Where it goes beyond the WTO in deepening and widening, it rarely goes very far. A number of features are specified which nowadays are also WTO accomplishments and where NAFTA was merely leading the way. Other arrangements are only marginally different from GATT rules, such as safeguards, customs valuation and intellectual property (TRIPs).

The implication for ASEAN is straightforward. ASEAN could come *close to what NAFTA has accomplished if* it would implement and comply with all the WTO codes that the ASEAN-6 have long committed to (CMLV could be given derogations with deadlines), and amend or go *beyond* them where it suits Southeast Asia for the two key properties of the AEC: a common production base and a single market. As to origin rules, AFTA/ASEAN is already doing better (i.e., less restrictive) and may further improve origin rules: it might move towards self-certification for bona fide MNCs with value chains inside ASEAN. If the AEC were tougher on removing NTMs other than technical regulations, intra-AEC market access need not differ much from that in NAFTA. However, this is a major 'if'. In IPRs, the TRIPs Agreement also matters for AEC countries and IPR cooperation may help to make the national regimes more robust. In anti-trust, ASEAN is no doubt far behind, and solid national competition policies (with basically no exceptions for sectors or privileged activities) are yet another attraction item for the confidence of MNCs in the proper functioning of local markets. On movement of business persons and/or mode 4 temporary entry, the AEC and NAFTA are now on similar tracks, with some progress needed for the AEC by 2015.

NAFTA is undoubtedly *more ambitious* than the AEC in three areas: investment, services and dispute settlement. All three are critical for the twin (instrumental) objectives of a common production base and a single market. All three require well-performing and credible legal systems in Member States. Credible dispute settlement, irrespective of the forms it might take (see item 13 in Table 5.1), requires independent panels with respected lawyers and full and unreserved compliance with their rulings. Appellate body reports or panel conclusions should simply not be passed through official AEC organs, implying bureaucratic or political approval; they ought to be treated like court rulings. The usual argument in ASEAN that its tradition is 'less confrontational' may be appropriate in diplomacy, but *not* for market transactions where private decisions implying private money or private efforts are based on public obligations or rights (e.g., of access etc.). In such cases, settlement of a dispute requires both full transparency and high quality judicial judgments. Doing it or 'approving' it behind closed doors by officials or politicians will ultimately throttle market initiatives to some extent due to arbitrariness or unpredictability. When it comes to investment and services, the cross-border opportunities in NAFTA are conditioned and far from general. In its own interest, ASEAN should thus be bolder in these two areas and negotiate suitable arrangements of its own, which, if credible and truly 'open', are bound to have favourable economic effects for FDI and services.

A critical lesson for ASEAN, already implicit in the four strategic choices of section 2.4, is NAFTA's firmness in accepting fully the corollary of credible liberalisation: one either centralises regulation and institutions (the EU model) to make that liberalisation credible; or one creates legal certainty about the extent of liberalisation with precision from the outset, together with the private and public instruments to defend one's (economic) rights and force commitments to be genuine. NAFTA chose the second option as, not unlike ASEAN, it has no interest in the EU model. The NAFTA logic and credibility for investors and business more generally is unassailable. NAFTA is successful because of the combination of substantive liberalisation beyond the WTO with credible domestic and joint legal arrangements and enforcement. For the AEC to emulate NAFTA would be of little avail if implementation and compliance were not credible, and the risks and costs for business strategies associated with the discretion of national governments cannot be foreseen in a rational way. The locational advantages that AEC is expected to generate, and the production base idea, would not be exploited to anywhere near potential. The single market idea would soon become a hollow phrase, which might even begin to backfire in terms of ASEAN's reputation. The preference for implicit deals and special arrangements, which often characterised past practice in many ASEAN countries, originates from episodes when liberalisation was far less prominent and less 'deep' while the MNCs coming to the region were fewer; the latter also had less choice. With value chains having become so important nowadays and the competitive climate so tough, the attraction will have to be built more on solid legal commitments and credible market-driven freedoms. Not only that, there is also a long-term risk that perennial (legal and institutional) weaknesses in the AEC, including at the country level in terms of implementation, may cause MNCs to get fed up and rearrange their value chains, given the extremely competitive climate in this respect. This will be easier the deeper and wider the East Asian integration process (which ASEAN favours so much) works out. By not accepting the corollary of deeper liberalisation, ASEAN would not only become less attractive but also more vulnerable to exit threats or actual exit.

One reason (among several) that the NAFTA treaty runs to 2,000 pages (including annexes) is the careful legislation about exceptions, some temporary, some indefinite. Here it is useful to realise that the exceptions are the inevitable byproduct of intrusive liberalisation principles, combined with credible compliance. Except for selective agricultural products (even so, intra tariffs are often zero and, if not, they have usually been reduced significantly), market access for goods is complete and for services (especially when seen as investment for local provision) is quite extensive. External tariffs tend to be low (there is no comparable case to the AFTA one of cars) and, where sensitive, intra-FTA free trade is not sacrificed. The 'solution' has been sought in restrictive origin rules hitting third countries which would otherwise exploit trade deflection. These restrictions can be regarded as negative from an economic welfare point of view. The AEC might, here and there, also have to accept a 'price' for fully-fledged liberalisation, although its outward-looking strategy might be a constraint.

Chapter 6

Options for the AEC and their practical implications

Having identified the strategic choices for a credible and effective AEC, and having made the economic case both for ASEAN as the 'production base' and for the AEC as a quasi-single market, the question is what are the options for the AEC? Three stylised options will be discussed. The purpose is to stimulate coherence in the AEC design and to identify priorities and trade-offs. Unlike Chapter 4, most details will be avoided. The three options are:

(1) a single-market-minus;
(2) ASEAN as a regional 'production base'; and
(3) AEC as a 'living' regional market and development compact.

6.1 The AEC as a single-market-minus

Understanding the AEC as a deeper and wider form of market integration is an obvious first option. Name and instruments like 'single market' (and its 'free flows') do suggest this forcefully. Our analysis of the Roadmap and its implementation (in Chapter 4) yields confusing signals. The Roadmap itself would seem to incorporate the right direction with respect to many chapters, but once one zooms in on the details, one finds numerous loose ends, occasional shallowness of cross-border liberalisation and a lack of commitment in several important components. However, its implementation does demonstrate a good deal of progress, too, expressed in new (binding) Agreements (such as ATIGA, ACIA, movements of natural persons, various on air transport, MRAs for professional services, etc.) – which is a significant turn for ASEAN given its traditions – and steady advances in sequential packages of implementation under AFAS, the customs programme and step-wise increasing market access for investment. There is criticism and some mistrust on the part of observers (including in the present project) because the AEC Scoreboard provides only superficial detail, whereas in deeper market integration what counts is precisely unconditional and transparent market access as well as effective implementation in the Member States.

Nevertheless, even here one should not draw hasty conclusions merely by comparing methods of implementation with those of the EU. There is indeed no doubt that implementation methods – including the indispensable surveillance (monitoring) of those national measures and a regime ensuring corrections in the AEC interest – in ASEAN are too weak for the purpose. It is far from easy, and perhaps even impossible, to combine extreme forms of intergovernmentalism (resulting from sensitivities about 'sovereignty') with effective regimes of implementation serving the common AEC interest properly. And this is not just a legal or institutional issue. If and insofar as the AEC is driven by the attractive economic motives as set out in section 2.5, bad implementation will simply cause such welfare gains to shrink to uninteresting magnitudes, that is, market forces will not react or only to a very limited extent. There now seems to be an increasing awareness that there is no escaping from these imperatives. The ASEAN Summit Declaration in Nay Pyi Taw of 11 May 2014 on the Realisation of the AEC by 2015 recognises, in item 11, that the ratification and implementation capacity of ASEAN Member States need to be strengthened. The Declaration also envisages (in item 12) 'to strengthen ASEAN institutions and mechanisms in order to further improve efficiency and effectiveness, taking into account the expansion of ASEAN activities ...'. In a way, the 2007 ASEAN Charter already encourages such strengthening but little actually happened. Rizal Sutma (2014) advocates to go back to the report of the ASEAN Eminent Persons on the draft Charter which specifies many improvements not having been included in the Charter. These notes by Dr Sutma are useful but nevertheless rather modest and possibly less than what is needed for AEC to succeed in markets and for fuelling growth. However, one should realise, too, that the *substance and scope* of implementation in the AEC is far less ambitious than in the EU: the cardinal difference is in positive integration. The EU routinely generates new or revised EU regulation, much of which is laid down in directives which require careful implementation in national law. The AEC will probably have only a very small fraction of this, which significantly reduces the implementation burden. Moreover, the EU uses more and more national institutions based on EU law, such as national sectorial regulators, assignments to national competition authorities or to networks of, say, national food safety authorities. Indeed, the EU resembles, much more than ASEAN ever will, a genuine two-tier government system of its Single Market. Nevertheless, for ASEAN to overcome the sensitivity of assigning the ASEAN Secretariat with effective monitoring tasks culminating in explicit and precise calls to correct national implementation, it should urgently search for other approaches which render the AEC more credible for business and citizens. One possibility is to decide, in common, to set up national watchdogs, organised in an ASEAN network routinely discussing implementation issues on a peer-pressure basis. ASEAN should accept that such watchdogs ought to remain outside government and be manned by independent lawyers and business, with government observers for purposes of reliable information and exchange. Their reporting should be public, of course, but purely factual. As long as the EDSM remains a defunct tool, and ACT remains insufficient, such national watchdogs can raise the credibility and transparency for business, while fostering better implementation of the AEC, without any supranational approach or 'hard' litigation against national governments as in NAFTA (or the EU).

The substantive weaknesses of the current single-market-minus approach for the AEC have become much clearer since Bali, and even more since the Roadmap was published. There is little point in reiterating the lengthy analysis from Chapters 3 and 4. In a number of domains and markets, the AEC will have to firm up the depth of its commitments, such as in several transport markets, equity limits of foreign (ASEAN) investment (the rule being 100 per cent, with limited exceptions) and greater commitment to the Single Customs Window. There is positive change here, with the completed ratification of the 2012 ASEAN Agreement on Customs and (finally) the signing, by six

ASEAN countries, in March 2015 of the Protocal on the Legal Framework to implement the single window. Ambitious but no less critical are the integration of financial markets – and with it, the construction of an ASEAN capital market in bonds and equity, giving a boost to investment possibilities – and the hopelessly delayed reduction or removal of 'core NTMs' as well as effective strategies to tackle TBTs. With respect to services, other than financial, the progress to date may be greater than expected. First, ASEAN's determination has to become firmer for a quasi-single market to be achievable. In network industry services, ASEAN should think again; so far, the approach has been splintered and largely ineffective. Perhaps, the ambition of a quasi-single market in such services is too far-fetched.

The single-market-minus will be achievable only if realistic deadlines are set (at least, 2020, if not later, for addressing, e.g., TBTs, several services, etc.); if transport liberalisation is taken more seriously; if NTBs are effectively addressed, beginning with 'core NTMs'; if financial services are able to follow the daunting agenda set for them (especially the positive integration agenda); and if the AEC Roadmap becomes firmer and more binding where it is now weak and unconvincing. ASEAN has to overcome its refusal (or allergy?) to consider positive integration; the signals are confusing in this respect. In any event, the fact is that ASEAN is still quite hesitant and tends to go for harmonisation only very sparingly. This is understandable, but there is a price: without it, the AEC will be less complete and less effective in economic terms as it will fail to lower trade costs in the wide sense of the word. In a similar vein, with the new agenda for financial services integration being so incredibly ambitious (see section 4.1.5), the degree of positive integration would need to reach much further than ASEAN might be able to muster. A quasi-single market must be credible or it simply will not be, and the region will end up at a lower stage of market integration compatible with its resolve to allow national autonomy to be retained.

6.2 ASEAN as a regional production base

Given the discussion in sections 2.5 and 4.3, it is more understandable why there seems to be no systematic approach to the notion of a 'production base' in the Roadmap or elsewhere. What is clear is that, especially for the middle income ASEAN countries, the attraction of segments of GVCs in and by itself is not necessarily the optimal policy. That might be suitable for the CMLV for a while. What matters for middle income ASEAN countries is the gradual migration towards higher value-added segments of GVCs in order to sustain a high growth path and avoid falling into the middle-income country trap. As noted, this is demanding in a number of ways, although a plain recipe cannot be given.

A first clear recommendation is openness in goods and services markets, that is, a single-market-minus is also good for the production base. Indeed, one can go further. Policymakers should learn to think of industrial 'activities' (in tasks) rather than in industrial sectors, but this is often difficult to change in trade policy. With the AEC going for a kind of single-market-minus anyway, this problem of adjusting trade policy systematically is at least no longer an issue inside ASEAN, and, if extended, less and less in East Asia. The liberalisation of services is a necessary but insufficient condition for doing well as a production base. When added-value in GVCs increases, so does the sophistication of services. Insofar as business services are concerned, ASEAN may well suffer from a high-skill shortage and this has to be addressed urgently. High skills in business services demand high quality universities, but almost certainly also an internationalisation strategy for the better students. There is also the question of trusted quality, calling for ways to recognise high-quality services, hence, going beyond merely liberalising any cross-border services. With respect to logistics – the most important 'trade costs' of GVCs – the core problem is infrastructure, both domestic and intra-ASEAN, immediately followed by the aspiration of efficient and consciously business-friendly customs. The domestic problem is not credible enough as an AEC question yet, because, ideally, the cross-border connections could be better dealt with by ASEAN. As noted, the potential gains in economic growth are even higher than the gains from the quasi-single-market! The latter (customs) is key for business and hardly less important for the single market, but progress has been slow.[1] It is worthwhile taking note of detailed and practical APEC work on what is called 'supply chain connectivity', lowering its costs and raising its quality (APEC 2013). The last, but by no means least, issue is

[1] See, for example, Inama and Sim (2013a) for the many obstacles before a Single Window will succeed in most ASEAN countries. But remember Figure 2.1 (in section 2.5) showing fairly high recent scores from business with regard to customs in the ASEAN-5.

the profound link with trade policy, especially vis-à-vis East Asia and possibly also other target markets. For the production base and GVCs, and much less for the single market aim as such, FTAs with East Asia are crucial. This is basically facilitating the emergence of a wider economic region where GVCs would move goods easily, but would not consider relocating too quickly. Indeed, GVCs might be attracted to locate even more of their facilities in the entire East Asia region as a smoothly run 'factory Asia'. These FTAs are often not 'deep', but this might change over time. Moreover, they already contain some similar ingredients to the AEC and they would seem to bolster the case to come and stay in East Asia. For ASEAN, connected with China, Japan and Korea (if not Taiwan), this is essential and likely to make it easier to argue that GVCs should establish themselves in the region as part of the same competitive 'neighbourhood'. Knowing that this extension of FTAs in the region would also help to boost the economic gains from exposure to competition (see Petri *et al.*, 2012), it is a rational priority to follow. The urgency to do this is further increased by a kind of competitive FTA race between RCEP, TPP, plans between China, Korea and Japan, and, finally, the EU's attempts to be better linked to East Asia as well.

Second, the investment dimension is absolutely critical for the production base. It is surprising and hardly consistent that the market access agenda in investment has been poorly specified as a ceiling of only 70 per cent being obligatory by the end of 2015. True, in goods sectors it tends to be higher factually (see section 4.1.4). Moreover, how open are ASEAN countries to multinationals – usually non-ASEAN –

because multinationals have to be attracted to the production base? It would seem that intra-ASEAN investment should in principle be free, with 100 per cent ownership, except in some sectors possibly, and with a review clause after X years. But whereas ASEAN has been able to define a common stance in trade policy vis-à-vis important trading partners, if the production base is so important, why not mimic this for world-class investors who bring the GVC segments or expand on them in one or more ASEAN countries? Finally, there is the question of whether ASEAN will be capable of pre-empting a subsidy or incentive war amongst its members, especially for investments bringing higher value-added segments of GVCs to the region. The AEC does not foresee any common competition policy, only an impetus to introduce national competition policy. However, those policies are concerned with anti-trust, not a common regime disciplining state aids in the region. Although a common regime may not be in the books for now, this issue will simply not go away, in particular, in a more distant future when average annual growth rates for the relevant ASEAN countries may begin to reduce somewhat.

The development dimension of the production base is rather ill-defined. Hence, a ragbag of suggestions is offered under 'competitive economic region' in Table 3.1, and a range of questions, which are pertinent for the production base, are posed in the single market part. However, the most important item is not AEC-driven at all: it is about the ever deeper 'integration' of GVC activities in the local economies via backward and forward linkages. Another way of saying this is that the domestic content of GVC exports is increasing over time due to local suppliers of inputs of goods and services, and to local purchases by other firms, including SMEs, or the public sector. The higher the value-added in GVCs, the greater the importance of knowledge capital (OECD 2013: 39–42), and this points to a crucial long-term strategy for all semi-developed or developed economies with respect to technical infrastructure, research and innovation. The AEC agenda cannot do much about this; it is the typical complementarity of long-term national development policy with the AEC calendar. Education and training for higher skills are equally important today as their effect in 'upgrading' might take another half a generation or more. ASEAN infrastructure is part and parcel of the competitive economic region, but these many masterplans, action plans and connectivity strategies show some ambivalence, as discussed above. Although it is vital to ensure early on that national infrastructure is connected with ASEAN and fills up 'missing links', there is a profound incentive problem with financing and bilateral or ASEAN-wide cooperation which risks having a paralysing effect on the pace of realising such works. ASEAN has stimulated a private infrastructure fund (of small size). Without any public initiatives of the appropriate scale, the optimal investment strategy in the region (exploiting cross-border spillovers effectively) is unlikely to be produced via market incentives which are solely interested in short pay-back periods and solid private returns. The wider returns dissipated in the ASEAN economy will not be captured by private investors, leading to significant underinvestment.

Altogether, the production base is a notion that hinges to a large extent on national initiatives and mere cooperative strategies. This also goes for strengthening IPRs. What ASEAN elements there are, are either items from what one could regard as a single market programme or common infrastructure visions which lack credible instruments to realise them anywhere near to what is desirable.

6.3 The AEC as a 'living regional market and development' compact

What binds ASEAN countries is the desire for socio-economic development in the region, besides some cultural, foreign policy and historical affinities, albeit with some painful hitches. What brings ASEAN even closer together nowadays is the presence of two emerging giants, India and China, each one more than double the size of ASEAN in terms of people and enjoying high rates of economic growth. This predicament drives the ASEAN economic agenda, even when this is rarely explicit. Development is not a zero-sum game, but ASEAN's open economy development strategy can be affected by competing giants in the wider region, for better or worse. Moreover, ASEAN countries have come to like secular high growth, not just growth. At first this was driven by the eradication of poverty, but that battle has been won by and large. With an example like Singapore in the group, and Japan, Korea, Taiwan and China in the wider region, growth expectations have become engrained in the ASEAN mindset. And a high-growth path will have to be followed even in the presence of the two giants, also caught in a long-term growth catch-up strategy of their own. This profound conviction in ASEAN has completely changed the thinking of ASEAN political leaders. Even just a year before the ASEAN Summit in Singapore in January 1992, there was no sign of any plan for an FTA. ASEAN was essentially foreign policy-oriented, in a selective fashion and with the famous 'ASEAN way' of consensual peer pressure, searching for what bound the countries and avoiding what might divide them. With the AFTA decision, first without a blueprint and with prudent conditional calendars and many opt-outs, ASEAN would change. Market integration is a subject very different from loose foreign policy and voluntary cooperation à la carte. Markets need certainty if business decisions are to be impacted for the common economic good. Gradually, ASEAN drifted into concluding binding agreements with a genuine 'bite', a novelty for ASEAN. AFTA soon became too shallow an exercise with too little effect on growth and development in the wider sense. After some experimentation with unconvincing and somewhat arbitrary calendars and programmes signed in ASEAN summits (Hanoi, Vientiane), but with no aim and no strategy behind it, the AEC was announced and sold as both a radical deepening and widening of AFTA, and as a strategy to help attract and upgrade GVCs to the region as a whole. The China factor clearly played a significant, but positive, role.[2] The message was unsurprising, except for its more visionary and radical form: ASEAN was to be a more homogeneous economic bloc, in the light of the dramatic transformation of Asia being led by two giants with growth ambitions. It could exploit its commonness far more for development purposes, in particular, by becoming more attractive for

[2] Note that the Chinese prime minister attended the Bali Summit and negotiations for an FTA framework agreement with China began soon after.

GVCs, in turn, linked to East Asia, with China as the leading engine.

This is how one could read the AEC Bali Declaration at the time, and even more so today. This option can be regarded as a mutually reinforcing two-pillar structure. However, whereas the single market idea requires a design based on market integration logic and has to be ASEAN-driven in every way, the production base notion lacks a stringent set of indispensable requirements, and the ASEAN elements of it tend to be more cooperative between the Member States or complementary but national. But the analogy of the two-pillar structure blocks a far more interesting perspective, namely, that of a *symbiosis* between the two. This is the option elaborated below.

What is probably best for ASEAN has been implicit in the Bali 'vision' right from the start, even if the design and the Roadmap have not brought this out systematically. The reason for this lack of coherence and rigorous logic can be traced back in the history of ASEAN, although it might be attributed as well to the enormous divergence in the group and the understandable hesitations to unconditionally sign up for the ambitious Bali concepts. Coherence and integration logic of the AEC will never be guided by the prior market access commitments as the EU has incorporated in its treaty and subsequent case law. But this does not mean that, over time, these consequences do not sink in. In ASEAN, given its determination to remain attractive for world investors and knowing the tremendous overall economic gains at stake, 'time' is a friend of coherence, deepening and widening. The present study has identified many instances where, in the decade since Bali, the AEC has become more committing and where initially soft plans or promises have been tightened and become more serious over time.

The AEC is therefore best regarded as a symbiosis of the single-market-minus and the production base, vague as the latter is and hinging more on national complementarity of sound socio-economic and education policies, besides research and technology and infrastructure. We have noted more than once that what is good for the single-market-minus is almost invariably also good for the production base. And complementarity of national policies (especially infrastructure) render the market integration framework far more effective. In this fashion, the AEC is best conceived as a 'living' compact between the ASEAN countries, for purposes of regional market integration and development. Moreover, it is equally crucial not to oversell the GVCs aspects of development. There are many economic activities which are not associated with GVCs, just as there are many aspects of indigenous economic development which, in the longer run, are crucial for development, too. The 'living' compact expresses a typical trait of ASEAN over time, policy convictions can be altered and commitments can be deepened, but the pace ought not to be forced and consensus matters. The highly competitive environment in East Asia, if not worldwide, and the high growth 'addiction' of all ASEAN developing countries, ensure that a sense of purpose will be maintained. The combination of the single market logic and the 'soft' but unassailable attraction of policy emulation inside ASEAN for the national development initiatives in the AEC agenda will generate further progress with more compelling coherence. What would be very helpful, however, would be a fundamental re-think when moving towards or beyond 2015.

The critical input for this re-think should be the November 2015 post-2015 programme for AEC until 2025, to be approved by the ASEAN Summit. An interesting report with numerous suggestions has been published by ERIA (2014).

This re-think should be based on ASEAN's own reformulation of this 'compact' now that some of its agenda has been achieved and the implications for deepening and widening of scope are better understood. It should improve the calendars of deadlines which remain too distant in the future and, in order to do that, first clarify what is part of the symbiosis and what is not. Ideally, it should also indicate how various national complementary policies relate to the common agenda. The present studies in the Integration through ASEAN Law project and the analysis as well as recommendations of the ERIA mid-term review of the Blueprint (ERIA 2012) could serve as a solid and wide-ranging starting point.

Chapter 7

Conclusions

The aim of the present monograph is to make the ASEAN economic integration model intelligible by applying a conceptual approach. The AEC combines two concepts: the ASEAN single market (which is likely to grow into its own *sui generis* notion of deeper market integration); and ASEAN as a production base for world multinationals, as well as more and more for ASEAN business itself (and which is ill-defined or not defined at all, not even when carefully checking the ASEAN Blueprint/Roadmap with some 300 items of concrete measures and milestones). The underlying strategic economic aim, which unites all ASEAN countries, is rapid and steady development, underpinned by long-term economic growth and an acceptance of gradual but secure structural change. The AEC can neither be understood conceptually nor practically without this overriding development and growth perspective in mind or, better, in the minds of the ASEAN political leaders.

The monograph takes a systematic look at these 'concepts', starting from the fundamentals of economic integration – which also matter for ASEAN – the Bali 'vision', and a scrutiny of the five instrumental instrumental objectives (free flows, single ASEAN market, ASEAN as production base, equitable development and its economic competitiveness), followed by a careful summary of the entire AEC Roadmap. This analysis is deepened for the first three of these five instrumental objectives by scrutinising implementation, that is, the substance of the commitments in the Roadmap in considerable depth, including progress to date. Interestingly, with the Roadmap only publicly available for less than seven years, one can already discern many instances where ASEAN has deepened its commitments and/or has made progress beyond what was originally drafted. The AEC has clearly inspired and stimulated strategic thinking in ASEAN Member States, and has prompted policy action over a wide front of policy domains. We show in several domains that ASEAN has improved its understanding of the full implications of such an ambitious strategy. However, in a conceptual approach, such 'good news' is less important than the verification of whether ASEAN is living up to the conceptual requirements of what a single market and/or ASEAN as a production base is or will be. The analysis of the progress towards a single market is easier in this respect, not only because the conceptual analysis is helped by a six-stage theory of market integration developed in section 2.2 – comprising two high stages akin to a single market – but also because of the instrumental objectives emphasised by ASEAN itself (in particular, the free flows). Our conclusion is, in short, that ASEAN will not enjoy free flows when studying today's calendars and follow-up commitments, but it is not excluded that – with some delay beyond 2015 – a single-market-minus might eventually develop. The current plans are, more often than not, ambivalent and the history of ASEAN, as well as its 'allergy' to even the slightest forms of centralisation or common regulation or harmonisation, does not sit comfortably with assumptions that ASEAN is ready or willing to develop the 'positive integration' to make that single-market-minus function properly and the free flows truly free. The ASEAN Summit Declaration of May 2014, quoted in section 6.1 with respect to critical institutional improvements, should be followed up in earnest in the 2015 Programme on the Roadmap to be decided in November 2015 by ASEAN leaders. And these intentions ought to be realised in actual practice. The routine objections of some in ASEAN that such moves would turn the AEC or ASEAN into a supranatural organisation, have no substance whatsoever. With better implementation obligations and slight centralisation on practical matters or follow-ups, it is still the ASEAN Member States running all major decisions in the region, but a lot of inefficiencies when dealing with detail, slowness in taking action and the lack of credibility in markets about genuine implementation and full transparency would be overcome. The November 2015 ASEAN Summit decisions on the post-2015 programme for the AEC are critical in this regard.

In goods markets, a number of weaknesses have survived in ATIGA and need to be addressed; still worse, the issue of 'core NTMs' and the removal or reduction of TBTs, already around for a long time, have not even begun to be taken seriously ten years after Bali and more than two decades after it was planned that the issues would be firmly resolved. In services, there are a number of inconsistencies and uncertainties; when zooming in on subdomains, one inevitably finds loose ends and 'flexibilities' (which means that national restrictions can be retained); the area of network industries' services is dealt with without much, if any, conviction, whereas transport protectionism inside ASEAN would seem to prevent much progress or at times prompts calendars with only far-distant commitments. In financial services, very little has happened – not surprising given the soft text in the

Roadmap – but 2013 suddenly brought to the surface a most ambitious and well-thought out strategy of financial market integration, together with an ASEAN capital market and solutions for demanding problems of financial stability in such a single market. However, the strategy being consistent and seemingly sound, implies that it is so ambitious that it would appear to be far out of bounds for the routine commitments of ASEAN even with the greater acceptance of common measures in the AEC. In investment, there is still no routine commitment to accept 100 per cent equity for foreign investors, although the production base idea strongly suggests that one wishes to attract precisely those world-class foreign investors. The free flow of skilled labour is highly conditional and carefully separated from the MRAs for professional services.

Our analysis has not been able to trace an operational definition of ASEAN as a production base. Moreover, many single-market-minus measures appear to serve, actually or potentially, the notion of this production base. However, a good many of the measures of the production base tend to be national, ranging from the business and investment climate to education, infrastructure (both domestic and cross-border), technical infrastructure for testing, standards, repairs and more generally the absorption of technology, and policies such as competition policy and consumer protection. It extends, of course, to the actual conduct of the customs for business, long a concern in ASEAN. Later in the monograph we undertake an attempt to exploit the recent empirical economics of global value chains to formulate an economic rationale for the production base approach by ASEAN, and it turns out to be a most interesting argument further strengthened by the determination of middle-income ASEAN countries to escape what is called the 'middle income trap'.

We attempt to provide critical ingredients for an ASEAN strategy underpinning the AEC, as this seems to be lacking and this omission is likely to severely hinder future developments. A careful comparison with NAFTA brings out a number of fundamental choices for ASEAN, both in institutional design and in terms of substance. It need not copy NAFTA, but the AEC does have to find consistent and workable alternatives in any event. An AEC strategy that is robust when the going gets more difficult – 2015 and beyond – should be based on a sound economic rationale, which we develop for two stylised scenarios: a cooperative ASEAN-led development strategy; and a pro-competitive single-market-minus for development. We find that both can be underpinned with powerful economic arguments which support the high growth perspectives of ASEAN leaders.

Three options are distinguished subsequently. One is the AEC as a single-market-minus, a very demanding but attractive option, not least because a lot of what is implied in this option would also be very useful for the production base. A second is ASEAN as a production base, with the important addition that the FTA character of ASEAN will increasingly disappear as ASEAN's production base becomes much more interesting as part of 'factory Asia' if deep FTAs with East Asia and some other trading partners can be concluded jointly for ASEAN as a single group. Nevertheless, the success of the production base for ASEAN's economic development hinges on a non-AEC property: the capability of individual ASEAN countries to develop backward and forward linkages with the local economy. The third one is really a symbiosis between the former two, not least in the light of the enormous pressures exercised by the catch-up growth of the two giants in the region: India and China. There is little doubt that, conceptually, such a symbiosis will not easily lead to coherence and consistency (never much of a characteristic of ASEAN), but one has to accept that this may improve over time, as before with AFTA. Indeed, time is a friend of coherence and deepening. One should regard the symbiosis as a 'living compact' for purposes of market integration and development, complemented by a range of national policies, often emulated between the ASEAN countries. In this sense, the Bali 'vision' may be rationalised after all and its more mature version might eventually be vindicated.

Executive summary

Understanding ASEAN's economic integration model is a genuine challenge. A fundamental reason why conceptual difficulties arise in the case of the ASEAN Economic Community (AEC) is that ASEAN architects observe two stylised (regional) economic integration approaches in the world which they do *not* want to pursue: the 'EU model', which is supranational, far too ambitious and also to a degree 'open-ended' in terms of further ambitions; and the classical free trade area (FTA) approach, even when upgraded a little nowadays. The AEC is based on two concepts, presented as 'parallel': the 'single market'; and ASEAN as a 'production base' for segments of global value chains. These two instruments have to be understood in the light of what matters most to ASEAN: the medium- or long-term growth prospect for the region. Thus, if the production base is expected to be growth-enhancing in a powerful way (as experience in East Asia suggests), the single market as a 'concept' may well be downgraded in actual practice. Since global value chains thrive on 'openness' of economies and easy market access (in particular, in East Asia), market access in East Asia via FTAs might rank as high or higher for the success of the ASEAN production base than the pursuit of an ever deeper – indeed, 'single' – internal ASEAN market. The present monograph focuses on the ASEAN economic integration logic from a conceptual point of view, but the intricate and multifold linkages with measures relevant for ASEAN as a 'production base' have explicitly been addressed as well.

The present contribution to the ASEAN Integration through Law project aims to scrutinise the concepts, logic, sequencing, coherence and options for the 2015 AEC. The author assumes an economic perspective, whilst taking due account of institutional, legal and political economy aspects. Economic integration processes largely take place in markets. Nevertheless, a political desire to pursue ever 'deeper' economic integration requires ever more demanding regulatory, economic policy, political and institutional as well as legal commitments by participating countries. This is bound to extend decision-making from trade (and 'ASEAN') ministers to broader government policies and reforms of standing economic regulation practices. Assuring 'deeper' economic integration is therefore very different in nature than fixing a classical FTA.

The AEC combines two concepts: the 'ASEAN single market', which is likely to grow into its own *sui generis* notion of deeper market integration; and ASEAN as a 'production base' for world multinationals as well as for ASEAN business itself (the latter is a most unclear concept, even when carefully checking the ASEAN Blueprint/Roadmap with some 300 items of concrete measures and milestones). The underlying strategic economic aim that unites all ASEAN countries is rapid and steady development, underpinned by long-term economic growth and an acceptance of gradual structural change. The monograph takes a systematic look at these 'concepts', starting from the fundamentals of economic integration – which also matter for ASEAN – ASEAN's four strategic choices about what FTA-plus to opt for (these choices are illustrated in a comparison with NAFTA), the economic rationale of the AEC, the Bali 'vision' and a scrutiny of the five instrumental economic concepts (free flows, single ASEAN market, ASEAN as production base, equitable development and its economic competitiveness). The economic rationale is developed for two stylised scenarios: a cooperative ASEAN-led development strategy and a pro-competitive single-market-minus serving development. This conceptual and economic foundation is followed by a careful summary of, and commentary on, the entire AEC Roadmap. Subsequently, this analysis is deepened for the first three of these five instrumental concepts by scrutinising the substance of the commitments in the Roadmap in considerable depth, including progress to date. Interestingly, even though the Roadmap became publicly available only in 2009, one can already discern many instances where ASEAN has deepened its commitments and/or made progress beyond what was originally drafted. The AEC has clearly stimulated strategic thinking in ASEAN Member States and prompted policy action over a wide front of policy domains. However, in a conceptual approach, such 'good news' is less important than the verification of whether ASEAN is living up to the conceptual requirements of what a single market and/or ASEAN as a production base is or will be. The analysis of the progress towards a single market is easier in this respect, not only because the conceptual analysis is helped by a six-stage theory of market integration developed in section 2.2 – comprising two high stages akin to a single market – but also because of the instrumental economic concepts emphasised by ASEAN itself (in particular, the 'free flows'). Our conclusion is that ASEAN will not enjoy free flows, when studying today's calendars and follow-up commitments, but it is not excluded that – with some delay beyond 2015 – a quasi-single market might eventually develop. The current plans are, more often than not, ambivalent and the history of ASEAN as well as its 'allergy' to even the slightest forms of centralisation or common regulation or harmonisation do not sit comfortably with the requirement that ASEAN is ready to develop the 'positive integration' to make that quasi-single market function properly and the free flows truly free.

In goods markets, a number of weaknesses have survived in ATIGA and need to be addressed. Far worse, the issue of 'core NTMs' and the removal or reduction of TBTs, already around for a long time, have not even begun to be taken seriously ten years after Bali. In services, there are a number of inconsistencies and uncertainties; when zooming in on subdomains, one inevitably finds loose ends and 'flexibilities' (i.e., national restrictions can be retained); the area of network industries' services is dealt with insufficiently and without much conviction, whereas transport protectionism inside ASEAN would seem to prevent much progress. In financial services, very little has happened – not surprising given the soft text in the Roadmap – but 2013 suddenly brought to the surface a most ambitious and well-thought out strategy of financial market integration, together with the pursuit of an ASEAN capital market and solutions for demanding problems of financial stability in such a single market. However, the strategy for financial market integration is so ambitious that it would appear far beyond the bounds of the routine commitments of ASEAN even with the greater acceptance of common measures in the AEC. In investment, there is still no routine commitment to accept 100 per cent equity for foreign investors, although the production base idea strongly suggests that one wishes to attract precisely those world-class foreign investors. The free flow of skilled labour is highly conditional and carefully separated from the MRAs for professional services.

Our analysis has been unable to trace an operational definition of ASEAN as a production base. Moreover, many quasi-single market measures also appear to serve, actually or potentially, the notion of this production base. However, a good many of the measures of the production base tend to be national, ranging from the business and investment climate to education, infrastructure (both domestic and cross-border), technical infrastructure for testing, standards, repairs and more generally the absorption of technology (which in turn hinges on high quality education), and policies such as competition policy and consumer protection. It extends to the actual conduct of the customs for business, long a concern in ASEAN. We undertake an attempt to exploit the recent empirical economics of global value chains to formulate an economic rationale for the production base approach by ASEAN, and it turns out to be a most interesting argument further strengthened by the determination of middle-income ASEAN countries to escape the 'middle income trap'.

We attempt to provide critical ingredients for an ASEAN strategy underpinning the AEC, as this seems to be lacking, an omission likely to severely hinder future developments. Apart from the four strategic choices when building an AEC (see above), we also compare the substance of NAFTA with the expected substance of the AEC (and the EU Single Market as a contrast). This detailed comparison helps one to appreciate the concrete implications of the present AEC design and hopefully clarifies the need for a well thought-out AEC strategy. ASEAN does not have to copy NAFTA and it can also go beyond it, but it must identify consistent and workable alternatives in any event. The two economic scenarios set out in section 2.5 indicate the beginnings of such a strategic reflection.

Three options are distinguished subsequently. One is the AEC as a single-market-minus, a very demanding but attractive option, not least because a lot of what is implied in this option would also be useful for the production base. A second is ASEAN as a production base. However, how much 'ASEAN' this really is remains unclear: ASEAN's production base is much more interesting as part of 'factory Asia' if deep FTAs with East Asia and some other trading partners can be concluded jointly for ASEAN as a single group. Nevertheless, the success of the production base for ASEAN's economic development hinges on a non-AEC property: the capability of individual ASEAN countries to develop backward and forward linkages with the local economy. The third one is really a symbiosis between the former two, not least in the light of the pressures emerging from the catch-up growth of the two giants in the region: India and China. Such a symbiosis does not easily lead to coherence and consistency, but this may improve over time, as before with AFTA. Indeed, time is a friend of coherence and deepening. One should regard the symbiosis as a 'living compact' for purposes of market integration and development, complemented by a range of national policies, often emulated between the ASEAN countries. In this sense, the Bali 'vision' may be rationalised after all and its more mature version might eventually be vindicated.

Appendix 1

The Balassa stages of economic integration

The Balassa stages of economic integration (1)

Stage	Definition	Characteristics/comments
Free trade area (FTA)	Tariffs and quotas abolished for imports from area members. Area members retain national tariffs (and quotas) against third countries.	Essence of GATT definition; no positive integration.
Customs union (CU)	Suppressing discrimination for CU members in product markets. Equalisation of tariffs (and no, or common, quotas) in trade with non-members.	Essence of GATT definition; no positive integration.
Common market (CM)	A CU that also abolishes restrictions on factor movements.	Is 'beyond' GATT; definition should also include services; no positive integration.

The Balassa stages of economic integration (2)

Stage	Definition	Characteristics/comments
Economic union	A CM with 'some degree of harmonisation of national economic policies in order to remove discrimination . . . due to disparities in these policies'.	Positive integration introduced; extremely vague.

(cont.)

Stage	Definition	Characteristics/comments
Total economic integration	'Unification of monetary, fiscal, social and counter cyclical policies.' 'Setting up of a supranational authority where decisions are binding for the Member States.'	Centralist; vision of unitary state; supranationality only introduced here.

Source: Pelkmans (2006: ch. 1).

REFERENCES

ADB Calculations (2010). *Asia 2050: Realizing the Asian Century.* Singapore.

ADB/ASEAN (2013). 'The Road to ASEAN Financial Integration', available at: www.adb.org/sites/default/files/pub/2013/road-to-asean-financial-integration.pdf.

Albada, R., J. Yap and P. Petri (2009). 'The AEC and Investment and Capital Flows', in M. Plummer and S. Y. Chia (eds), *Realizing the ASEAN Economic Community.* Singapore: ISEAS, pp. 83–115.

Albert, M. and R. Ball (1983). 'Towards European Recovery in the Eighties', European Parliament Working Part Document 1983/83, Luxembourg, July.

Athukorala, P. (2010) 'Production Networks and Trade Patterns in East Asia: Regionalization or Globalization?' ADB Working Paper No. 56

Anderson, G. (ed.) (2012). *Internal Markets and Multi-level Governance.* Toronto: Oxford University Press.

APEC (2013). *The 2013 Interim Assessment for Supply Chain Connectivity Framework Action Plan.* Singapore: APEC Policy Support Unit, March.

ASEAN (2010). *Roadmap for the ASEAN Community 2009–2015.* Jakarta: ASEAN Secretariat.

(2012). *ASEAN Economic Community Scorecard.* Jakarta, ASEAN Secretariat.

Atkins, W. (1997). *Technical Barriers to Trade,* Single Market Review, Subseries III.1, Office of Official Publications of the EC, Luxembourg. London: Kogan Page.

Balassa, B. (1961). *The Theory of Economic Integration*. Homewood, IL: Irwin.

(1976). 'Types of Economic Integration', in F. Machlup (ed.), *Economic Integration Worldwide, Regional, Sectoral*. London: Macmillan, pp. 17–31.

Beckman, B., L. Bernard, R. Yusran and H. L. Tan (2013). 'Dispute Settlement, Critical Analysis of Existing Instruments', monograph for the ASEAN Integration through Law project.

Bergsten, F. (1995). 'Competitive Liberalisation and Global Free Trade', Working Paper 96/15, Institute of International Economics, Washington DC.

Blind, K. (2004). *The Economics of Standards*. Cheltenham: Edward Elgar.

Cadot, O., M. Malouche and S. Saez (2012). *Streamlining Non-tariff Measures: A Toolkit for Policy-makers*. Washington DC: World Bank.

Cadot, O. and M. Malouche (eds) (2012). *Non-tariff Measures: A Fresh Look at Trade Policy's New Frontier*. Washington DC: World Bank/CEPR.

Chen, N. (2004). 'Intra-national versus International Trade in the EU: Why do National Borders Matter?' *Journal of International Economics*, 63(1): 93–118.

Chesterman, S. and A. Yusuf (2013). 'ASEAN Instruments of Monitoring', monograph for the ASEAN Integration through Law project.

Chia, S. Y. (2007). 'ASEAN and Narrowing the Development Gap', in H. Soesastro and J. Joewono (eds), *The Inclusive Regionalist, A Festschrift for Jusuf Wanandi*. Jakarta: CSIS, pp. 319–35.

(2011). 'ASEAN's Economic Integration: Developments and Challenges', *Asian Economic Policy Review*, 6: 43–63.

(2014). 'Towards Freer Movement of Skilled Labour in AEC 2015 and Beyond', ERIA Policy Brief No. 2014-02, May.

Chia, S. Y. and M. Plummer (2013). 'Advancing ASEAN Economic Integration: Assessing the AEC and its Challenges', monograph for the ASEAN Integration through Law project.

Cooper, C. and B. Massell (1965) 'A New Look at Customs Union Theory', *Economic Journal*, 75: 742–7

Cremona, M., D. Kleimann, J. Larik, R. Lee and P. Vennesson (2013). 'Collectively ASEAN: An Inventory and Typology of ASEAN External Agreements', monograph for the ASEAN Integration through Law project.

Correia de Brito, A. and J. Pelkmans (2012). 'Pre-empting Technical Barriers in the Single Market', CEPS Policy Brief No. 277, Brussels, July, available at: www.ceps.eu.

Davidson, P. (2004). 'The ASEAN Way and the Role of Law in ASEAN Economic Cooperation', *Singapore Yearbook of International Law*, 8: 165.

De Backer, K. (2011). 'Global Value Chains: Selected Policy Issues', Chengdu, 18 October (slides).

(2013). 'OECD Work on Global Value Chains and Trade in Value Added', Bruegel workshop, Brussels, 27 June (slides).

Dee, Ph. (2005). 'A Compendium of Barriers to Services Trade', study prepared for the World Bank, Australian National University, Canberra.

(2009a). *What Behind-the-Border Reforms in Services and Investment are Best Done through Trade Agreements?* Canberra: ANU, April.

(2009b). *Services Liberalization toward the AEC.* Canberra: ANU.

(2010). 'Deepening East Asian Economic Integration in Services', ERIA Policy Brief No. 2010–01, October.

(2015). 'Monitoring the Implementation of Services Trade Reform towards an ASEAN Economic Community', ERIA Discussion Paper No. 2015–44, May.

Dehousse, R. and D. Aziz (2013). 'The Instruments of Governance of ASEAN', monograph for the ASEAN Integration through Law project.

Delgado, J. (2006). 'Single Market Trails Home Bias', Bruegel Policy Brief No. 5, Brussels, available at: www.bruegel.org.

Dios, L. de (2004). 'Issues and Options for the Work Programme to Eliminate NTBs in AFTA', Manila/Jakarta/Brussels, APRIS/ASEAN programme, September.

Ehlermann, C. (1986). 'The Internal Market following the Single European Act', *Common Market Law Review*, 24: 361–409.

Eichengreen, B., D. Park and K. Shin (2013). 'Growth Slowdowns Redux: New Evidence on the Middle Income Trap', NBER Working Paper No. 18673.

Engel, Ch. and J. Rogers (2004). 'European Product Market Integration after the Euro', *Economic Policy*, 18, July.

ERIA (2012). 'Mid-term Review of the Implementation of the AEC Blueprint', Executive Summary, Jakarta, p. 51, available at: www.eria.org/Mid-Term%20Review%20of%20the%20Implementation.

(2014) 'ASEAN Rising: ASEAN and AEC Beyond 2015', Jakarta, available at: www.eria.org/publications/key_reports/ASEAN-Rising.html.

Ethier, W. (1998). 'Regionalism in a Multi-lateral World', *Journal of Political Economy*, 106: 6.

European Commission (1996). 'Economic Evaluation of the Internal Market' (Monti Report), European Economy, Reports and Studies No. 4, European Commission, Brussels, December.

(2011). 'Towards a Better Functioning Single Market for Services: Building on the Results of the Mutual Evaluation Process of the Services Directive', COM(2011) 20, 27 January 2011, European Commission, Brussels.

(2012). 'The Economic Impact of the Services Directive, A First Assessment following Implementation', DG EcFin, Economic Papers No. 456, June, European Commission, Brussels.

(2013) 'Market Functioning in Network Industries – Electronic Communications, Energy and Transport', DG EcFin, Occasional Papers No. 129, February, European Commission, Brussels.

Ewing-Chow, M. (2008). 'Culture Club or Chameleon: Should ASEAN Adopt Legalization for Economic Integration?' *Singapore Yearbook for International law*, 12: 225–37.

Farole, T. (2011). 'Special Economic Zones: What Have We Learned?' VOXEU, 27 May 2013, available at: www.voxeu.org.

Geradin, D. (2006). 'Twenty Years of Liberalization of Network Industries: Where Do We Go Now?' Tilburg University, Inaugural lecture, 3 November.

Gill, I. and H. Kharas (2007). *An East Asian Renaissance*. Washington DC: World Bank.

Goldberg, P. and F. Verboven (2005). 'Market Integration and Convergence to the Law of One Price: Evidence from the European Car Market', *Journal of International Economics*, 65: 49–73.

Hatzopoulos, V. (2012). *Regulating Services in the EU*. Oxford University Press.

Head, K. and T. Mayer (2000). 'Non-Europe: The Magnitude and Causes of Market Fragmentation in Europe', *Weltwirtschaftliches Archiv (Review of World Economics)*, 136(2): 285–314.

Hew, D., M. Pangestu, J. Pelkmans and H. Soesastro (2004). 'Outline Perspective Plan for the ASEAN Economic Community', unpublished study for the ASEAN Secretariat, Jakarta, August.

Hocking, R. (1980). 'Trade in Motorcars between the Major European Producers', *Economic Journal*, 90: 1.

Ilzkovitz, F. *et al.* (2007). 'Steps Towards a Deeper Economic Integration, a Contribution to the Single Market Review', DG EcFin Economic Papers No. 271, January.

Inama, S. and E. Sim (2013a). 'Legal and Policy Foundations of the AEC', monograph for the ASEAN Integration through Law project.

(2013b). 'Disentangling Rules of Origin in ASEAN External Relations', monograph for the ASEAN Integration through Law project.

Ing, L. Y. and S. Magiera (2015). 'Business Licensing: A Key to Investment Climate Reform', ERIA Discussion Paper No. 2015–5.

Ishida, M. (2009). 'Special Economic Zones and Economic Corridors', ERIA Discussion Papers, ERIA-DP-2009-16, June.

Ishido, H. and Y. Fukunaga (2012). 'Liberalization of Trade in Services: Toward a Harmonized ASEAN++FTA', ERIA Policy Brief 2012–02, March.

Johnson, H. (1965). 'An Economic Theory of Protectionism, Tariff Bargaining and the Formation of Customs Unions', *Journal of Political Economy*, 73(6): 256–283.

Kleimann, D. (2013). 'Beyond Market Access? The Anatomy of ASEAN's Preferential Trade Agreements', EUI Working Papers, LAW 2013/1, European University Institute, Florence.

Kuijper, P., J. Mathis, N. Morris and P. Govindasamy (2013). 'Towards an ASEAN Model External Agreement', monograph for the ASEAN Integration through Law project.

Landingin, N. and D. Wadley (2005). 'Export Processing Zones and Growth Triangle Development: The Case of the BIMP-EAGA, South East Asia', *Journal of International Development*, 17(1): 67–96.

Lee, C. and Y. Fukunaga (2013). 'ASEAN Regional Cooperation on Competition Policy', ERIA Discussion Paper 2013–03, April.

Lloyd, P. (2005). 'What is a Single Market? An Application to the Case of ASEAN', *ASEAN Economic Bulletin*, 22(3): 251–65.

Manchin, M. and A. Pelkmans-Balaoing (2008). 'Clothes Without an Emperor: Analysis of the Preferential Tariffs in ASEAN', *Journal of Asian Economics*, 19: 213–23.

Mayer, F., P. Mavroidis, K. Alter and L. Helfer (2013). 'Comparative Toolbox of Dispute Mechanisms', monograph for the ASEAN Integration through Law project.

McKinsey (2003). 'ASEAN Competitiveness Study', report for the ASEAN Secretariat, Jakarta.

Mustilli, F. and J. Pelkmans (2012). 'Securing EU Growth from Services', CEPS Special Report No. 67, Brussels, June, available at: www.ceps.eu.

(2013). 'Access Barriers to Services Markets: Mapping, Tracing, Understanding and Measuring', CEPS Special Report No. 77, Brussels, available at: www.ceps.eu.

Narjoko, D. (2015). 'AEC Blueprint Implementation Performance and Challenges: Non-Tariff Measures and Non-Tariff Barriers', ERIA Discussion Paper 2015–39, May.

Narjoko, D., P. Kartika and T. Wicaksono (2009). 'Narrowing the Development Gap in ASEAN', in M. Plummer and S. Y. Chia (eds), *Realizing the ASEAN Economic Community*. Singapore: ISEAS, pp. 116–41.

Nitsch, V. (2000), 'National Borders and International Trade: Evidence from the EU', *Canadian Journal of Economics*, 22(4): 1091–105.

OECD (2013). 'Interconnected Economies, Benefiting from Global Value Chains', Synthesis Report, OECD, Paris, May.

Orefice, G. and N. Rocha (2011). 'Deep Integration and Production Networks: An Empirical Analysis', WTO Staff Working Paper No. ERSD-2011-11.

Pacchioli, C. (2011). 'Is the EU Internal Market Suffering from an Integration Deficit? Estimating the "Home Bias" Effect', CEPS Working Document No. 348, available at: www.ceps.eu.

Pelkmans, J. (1980). 'Economic Theories of Integration Revisited', *Journal of Common Market Studies*, 18: 4.

(1985). 'The Institutional Economics of European Integration', in M. Cappeletti, J. Weiler and M. Seccombe (eds), *Integration Through Law: Europe and the American Federal Experience, vol. I: Methods, Tools, and Institutions*. New York and Berlin: de Gruyter, pp. 318–96.

(1987a). 'Preventing a Trench War: Removing Technical Barriers in Europe and Lessons for ASEAN', in N. Sopiee *et al.* (eds), *ASEAN at the Crossroads*. Kuala Lumpur: ISIS, pp. 489–510.

(1987b). 'The New Approach to Technical Harmonisation and Standardisation', *Journal of Common Market Studies*, 25: 3.

(1987c). 'Alternative Methods of Economic Integration, in N. Sopiee *et al.* (eds), *ASEAN at the Crossroads*. Kuala Lumpur: ISIS, pp. 421–36.

(1995), 'Comment', in A. Sykes (ed.), *Product Standards in Integrated Goods Market*. Washington DC: Brookings Institution, pp. 154–68.

(1999). 'Southeast Asian Puzzles in International Organization', in W. van Genugten *et al.* (eds), *Realism and Moralism in International Relations*. The Hague and New York: Kluwer Law, pp. 107–28.

(2001). 'Making EU Network Markets Competitive', *Oxford Review of Economic Policy*, 17: 3.

(2006). *European Integration, Methods and Economic Analysis*, 3rd edn. Harlow: Prentice Hall.

(2007). 'Mutual Recognition in Goods. On Promises and Disillusions', *Journal of European Public Policy*, 14(5): 699–716.

(2008). 'Economic Concept and Meaning of the Internal Market', in J. Pelkmans, D. Hanf and M. Chang (eds), *The EU Internal Market in Comparative Perspective*. Brussels and New York, Peter Lang, pp. 29–76.

(2011). 'European Union Single Market: Design and Development', *New Palgrave Dictionary of Economics*, December, available at: www.dictionaryofeconomics.com.

(2012a). 'The European Union (Single Market)', in G. Anderson (ed.), *Internal Markets and Multi-level Governance*. Toronto: Oxford University Press, pp. 77–101.

(2012b). 'Mutual Recognition, Economic and Regulatory Logic in Goods and Services', in T. Eger and B. Schaefer (eds), *Research Handbook on the Economics of EU Law*. Cheltenham: Edward Elgar, pp. 113–45.

Pelkmans, J. and P. Brenton (1998). 'Bilateral Trade Agreements with the EU: Driving Forces and Effects', in O. Memedovic *et al.* (eds), *Multilateralism and Regionalism in the Post Uruguay Round Era*. Cheltenham: Edward Elgar, pp. 87–120.

Pelkmans, J. and A. Correia de Brito (2012). *Enforcement in the EU Single Market*, Brussels, CEPS, October, available at: www.ceps.eu.

Pelkmans, J. and G. Luchetta (2013). 'Enjoying the Single Market for Network Industries', Paris, Notre Europe, Studies and Reports No. 95, February, available at: www.notre-europe.eu.

Pelkmans, J. and F. Mustilli (2013). 'A Moving Target: EU's Trade Strategy towards ASEAN', briefing paper for the INTA Committee of the European Parliament, April, available at: www.europarl.europa.eu.

Pelkmans, J. and A. Renda (2011). 'Single eComms Market? ... No Such Thing', *Communications & Strategies*, No. 82.

Pelkmans-Balaoing A., (2013). 'The Middle-Income Country Trap: Definitions, Indicators, Challenges', April, available at: www.EMIT-project.net.

Peng, L., S. Hix and S. Chalermpalanupap (2013). 'Institution and Decision-making Processes: Inventory and Critical Analysis', monograph for the ASEAN Integration through Law project.

Petri, P., M. Plummer and F. Zhai (2012). 'ASEAN Economic Community: A General Equilibrium Analysis', *Asian Economic Journal*, 26(2): 93–118.

Piris, J. and W. Woon (2013). 'An Exploration of the Role and Constraints of the ASEAN Secretariat Legal Division', monograph for the ASEAN Integration through Law project.

Plummer, M. and S. Y. Chia (eds) (2009). *Realizing the ASEAN Economic Community: A Comprehensive Assessment*. Singapore: ISEAS.

Prassetya, R. and P. Intal (2015). 'AEC Blueprint Implementation and Challenges: Standards and Conformance', ERIA Discussion Paper 2015-42, May.

Pupphavesa, W., S. Chiasrisawatsuk, S. Sutsawads and S. Ongkittikul (2009). 'Competition Policy, Infrastructure, and Intellectual Property Rights', in M. Plummer and S. Y. Chia (eds), *Realizing the ASEAN Economic Community*. Singapore: ISEAS, pp. 58–82.

Quah, J. *et al.* (2013). 'Governance and Management, the Member States' Apparatus: An Inventory and Critical Analysis', monograph for the ASEAN Integration through Law project.

Rashid, Z., F. Zhai, P. Petri, M. Plummer and S. Y. Chia (2009). 'Regional Market for Goods, Services and Skilled Labour', in M. Plummer and S. Y. Chia (eds), *Realizing the ASEAN Economic Community*. Singapore: ISEAS, pp. 20–57.

Reyes, V. (2013). 'Implementation of the ASEAN Cosmetics Directive in the Philippines', monograph for the ASEAN Integration through Law project.

Sapir, A. (2011). 'European Integration at the Crossroads: A Review Essay on the 50th Anniversary of Bela Balassa's Theory of Economic Integration', *Journal of Economic Literature*, XLIX(4): 1200–29.

Sauve, P., D. Neo and D. Streho (2013). 'Liberalization of Trade in Services under the ASEAN Framework Agreements in Services', monograph for the ASEAN Integration through Law project.

Sukma, R. (2014), 'ASEAN Beyond 2015: The Imperatives for Further Institutional Change', ERIA Policy Brief 2014-05, August.

Swann, P. (2010). 'The Economics of Standardization: An Update', report for the Department of Business, Innovation and Skills, London.

Sykes, A. (ed.) (1995). *Product Standards in Integrated Goods Markets*. Washington DC: Brookings Institution.

Tan, K. and Ph. Dann (2013). 'The Role of Law in the ASEAN Project: Potential and Constraints', monograph for the ASEAN Integration through Law project.

Thio, L. and I. Venzke (2013). 'The Internal Effect of ASEAN External Relations and its Impact on the Legal Order of ASEAN', monograph for the ASEAN Integration through Law project.

Tinbergen, J. (1954). *International Economic Integration*. Amsterdam and New York: North Holland.

(1956). *Economic Policy: Principles and Design*. Amsterdam: North Holland.

UNCTAD (2010). *Non-tariff Measures: Evidence from Selected Developing Countries and Future Research Agenda*. Geneva: UNCTAD.

(2013). *World Investment Report 2013*. Geneva: UNCTAD, June.

Urata, S. and M. Ando (2009). 'Investment Climate Study on ASEAN Member Countries', in S. Urata and M. Okabe (eds), *Tracing the Progress towards the AEC*, ERIA Research Project Report 2009-3, Jakarta, pp. 125–89.

Urata, S. and M. Okabe (eds) (2011). 'Overview' in *Toward a Competitive ASEAN Single Market: Sectoral Analysis*', ERIA, available at: www.eria.org.

Whalley, J. (1996). 'Why do Countries Seek Regional Trade Agreements?' NBER Working Paper No. 5552.

Weiler, J. (2013). 'The Role of Member States' Jurisdictions in Enhancing the Rule of Law', monograph for the ASEAN Integration through Law project.

Weiler, J. and M. Ewing-Chow (2013). 'A Differentiated Approach to ASEAN Compliance and Dispute Settlement', monograph for the ASEAN Integration through Law project.

Wihardja, M. (2014). 'Financial Integration Challenges in ASEAN Beyond 2015', ERIA Policy Brief 2014–08, August.

Wilson, J. (1995). *Standards and APEC: An Action Agenda.* Washington DC: Institute of International Economics.

WTO/JETRO (2010). 'Trade Patterns and Global Value Chains in East Asia: From Trade in Goods to Trade in Tasks', WTO, Geneva, available at: www.wto.org.

WTO (2012). *World Trade Report 2012, Trade and Public Policies: A Closer Look at Non-tariff Measures in the 21st Century*, Geneva: WTO, available at: www.wto.org.

Yamano, N., B. Meng and K. Fukasaku (2011). 'Fragmentation and Changes in the Asian Trade Network', ERIA Policy Brief No. 2011-01, January, available at: www.eria.org.

INDEX

Lightning Source UK Ltd.
Milton Keynes UK
UKOW07f2234030716

277541UK00001B/1/P